The Lives of Teacher Educators

The Lives of
Teacher Educators

Edward R. Ducharme

FOREWORD BY HARRY JUDGE

Teachers College, Columbia University
New York and London

Published by Teachers College Press, 1234 Amsterdam Avenue,
New York, NY, 10027

Library of Congress Cataloging-in-Publication Data

Ducharme, Edward R.
    The lives of teacher educators / Edward R. Ducharme : foreword by
  Harry Judge.
      p.   cm.
    Includes bibliographical references (p.   ) and index.
    ISBN 0-8077-3257-5 (alk. paper)
    1. Teacher educators – United States – Attitudes. 2. Teachers
  colleges – United States – Faculty. I. Title.
LB1778.2.D83 1993   93-19212
370.73 – dc20

Printed on acid-free paper

Manufactured in the United States of America

99 98 97 96 95 94 93   8 7 6 5 4 3 2 1

Contents

Foreword

Writing forewords to books written by others is a dangerous business. The opposing perils are represented by Piety and Sourness. A pious foreword—one that says simply that what follows is indeed a good book—deserves to be skipped and should therefore not have been written in the first place. Sour ones, which, in the manner of some reviews, pick holes in the text (and by implication suggest that the reviewer could have written a much better book), are equally inappropriate. My problem is that I do wish enthusiastically to commend the chapters that follow, and yet to argue that the reader would be wise to question the author's conclusions on several important points. It is clear that the author will appreciate such honest dissent. Even more important, one of the many virtues of this valuable study is that it does scrupulously separate the evidence from the analysis and so leaves the reader free to draw other conclusions.

One reason for asking a European to write a note introducing a work by an American scholar is, presumably, to sharpen such differences of interpretation and emphasis. The School of Education does remain a distinctively North American phenomenon, and is for that reason too easily taken for granted. Many of the issues raised in these pages look very different when addressed by, say, a Frenchman or a German. Underlying many of the correct assumptions in this book are concepts of the role of the teacher, the structure of the university, and even the purposes of society. This Introduction will deliberately choose an outsider's view on such matters. Even an insider reading these seven chapters will need to keep in mind the place of the teacher educator, as the author carefully defines that term, in a world that is also inhabited by Arts and Science faculty and by school personnel, as well as by specialists in administration and counselling psychology within the Schools of Education themselves. All of these are important connections. It is made clear at the outset that this is a study relevant neither to all those somehow engaged in the education of teachers nor to all those whose lives are embraced by the School of Education. Equally important and illuminating would be a contrastive study placing the lives of those who are involved in teacher education (narrowly defined) against the experience of those working within higher education in other professional schools—social work as much as business.

This is a refreshingly optimistic book. The interviews of thirty-four faculty members (twelve of them women) in eleven institutions are mined to produce a composite portrait of a man or woman who in the past enjoyed school teaching, feels generally at home in higher education, has a sense of pleasure and even excitement in the daily tasks of the trade, welcomes and respects students, and maintains a potent sense of idealism. The case is well argued, but the reader left free to take the evidence in other ways. A comparative perspective would, I suspect, moderate the optimism.

A successful French woman academic (to choose deliberately an illuminating point of vision) would read that most of the faculty studied here went into teaching in a somewhat casual if not absent-minded way, assisted by the absence of high entrance standards or vigorous competition. They quite enjoyed what they did, liked the human contacts but expressed no enthusiastic interest in the subject-matter of what they were presumably teaching, and left the schools after five years or so, never to return. Moreover, they left school teaching precisely because it was a professionally flat and undemanding career, dominated by routine, whereas work in a university or college gave them much more leisure and less supervision. Of course, there were new demands and pressures, notably to "do research" and to publish, but this seems a small price to pay: "I've got about 250 things in print; the vitae's about 25 pages long." At no point is there any vision, intellectual or moral, of what the research in such institutions might or should be about, nor of how it might improve the lives and learning of children, nor contribute to a powerful intellectual tradition: "I just love to see my name in print." The real satisfactions lie in working in gentle and hassle-free environments where colleagues are uncritical of one another, and in experiencing a warm sense of doing some good.

The author, then, should hardly be surprised or disappointed when so many of his subjects have hardly heard of the Holmes Group or (in response to what he wisely identified as a key question) observe "I read *about* books more than I read books." The Bible, Macbeth, *Horace's Compromise*, and "the handbook" (which turns out to be Wittrock) scarcely compose a bibliography for a learned profession. It may indeed be that, in so many subtle ways, some of the experience of the twelve women does point toward the reality of implicit oppression. But what would the hardheaded French woman academic make of a professor who is overwhelmed by 110 advisees? "Yeah, I've been told to shut the door and do my writing.

But maybe it's my elementary school background, but I just can't do that." Or of one who complained of a lack of mentorship because "No one told me that the *Chronicle of Higher Education* was the place to look for a job"?

So much for the French guest I have impertinently intruded into these paragraphs. We need to understand a great deal more of the lives of teacher educators, if only to avoid the pain of having to read about their collective death. This study is of importance in advancing such work, in provoking the reader to make private interpretations of the rich evidence offered, and—in the final pages—in pointing towards the further studies that are so urgently needed.

Harry Judge
Oxford

The Lives of Teacher Educators

1 The Study of Teacher Educators

*Historically, functionally, and legally, the education professoriate is se-
cure within the academic firmament. The preparation of teachers is as
vital to society's perpetuation as any other professional preparation program. Schools, colleges, and departments of education are as much a
part of the campus scene as departments of history, chemistry, or other
disciplines. Education is hardly a minor profession. Despite decades of
both legitimate and unfounded criticisms, the education professoriate
has survived and thrived.*

— Wisniewski & Ducharme, 1989a, p. 147

These are brave words about an embattled faculty group that has
lacked a complete description in the literature of higher education. In this
book, using material from interviews with 34 individuals, I describe teacher education faculty more comprehensively than previous writers have
done, provide an enriched understanding of their personal lives and professional careers, indicate how they perceive themselves, and set their place
more firmly in the higher education hierarchy. Through an examination
of particular lives of teacher educators, I will substantiate one of the themes
of the above quotation: that education faculty, and by implication, teacher
education faculty, are part of the "academic firmament," a place they have
not always held.

This book also informs the study of higher education faculty generally, an area of considerable scholarly activity and interest (Russell, Cox,
Williamson, Boismier, Javitz, Fairweather, & Zimbler, 1990). Ladd and
Lipset (1975), Rudolph (1962), Clark (1987), and Wilson (1979) are but
a few of the authors who have written on higher education faculty. The
major foci of these and other scholars are the faculty teaching the traditional, major disciplines of the academy. Education faculty are rarely focal
points in these works.

An example of the genre is Burton R. Clark's *The Academic Life: Small Worlds, Different Worlds* (1987), a study of contemporary academic life preceded by a thoughtful history of the professoriate in America. Clark bases his analysis of American higher education on his interviews with and observations of faculty from physics, biology, political science, English, business, and medicine, thus combining four of the traditional academic disciplines with two of the most entrepreneurial. He interlaces quotations from 170 interviews that preceded the writing of the book with his own descriptions and analyses, a technique similar to that which I have employed in this work. The quotations illuminate and enlarge his points of view.

Clark's focus on the faculty from the disciplines he chose automatically results in little analysis of education faculty; on the few occasions when he writes about education faculty, he quotes what professors in *other* disciplines say about them. For example, he quotes from several faculty employed at state universities, former normal schools or state teachers colleges with holdover "education" personnel serving in administrative and teaching roles, in some instances provoking resentment over the influence of "education people" (p. 167).

One learns little about education faculty from Clark's work or from the work of other writers on higher education, not a surprising situation, given the marginal importance of education units at many institutions and customary academic snobbery. Agne and I even referred to education faculty as aliens: "Latecomers to the academic game, professors of education are often seen as aliens in a strange land" (Ducharme & Agne, 1982, p. 30). Clifford and Guthrie (1988) also refer to education faculty as "marginal men, aliens in their own worlds" (p. 3). Much of the literature on higher education faculty treats education faculty lightly or ignores them totally. Clark's brief comments on education faculty well illustrate their dilemma of often being *in* higher education but not always being *of* it.

A PROBLEM OF DEFINITION

Education faculty are rarely the subject of sustained study, teacher education faculty even more rarely so. Given the structure of higher education, it is difficult to identify who the teacher educators are. The problems of identification and definition are compounded by the number and variety of individuals involved in teacher education and the reluctance of some education faculty to identify themselves as teacher educators even though they are much involved in teacher education. Institutional mission or faculty perception of institutional mission may account for some of the reluctance: "At major private institutions, 71.6% [of education faculty] say that preparing teachers is of considerable importance, but only 11.9% see preparing teachers as essential for tenure" (Soder, 1990, p. 706). Teacher education is "done" by a wide variety of professionals: cooperating teachers in the lower schools (elementary and secondary schools), faculty in arts and sciences who teach content courses to teacher education students, state department of education personnel who conduct workshops, and a number of others, virtually none of whom call themselves teacher educators.

Even education faculty who spend the major portion of their time with the teacher education curriculum and students often do not identify themselves as teacher educators. For example, in the 1987 Committee on Research About Teacher Education (RATE) survey sponsored by the American Association of Colleges for Teacher Education (AACTE) and conducted at nearly 90 institutions, less than 30% of faculty teaching the secondary methods courses identified themselves as teacher educators (American Association of Colleges for Teacher Education, 1987). Schneider (1987) observes that

> Although schools of education are often viewed by the university community as the place where they train teachers, only a proportion of faculty members, students and alumni identify themselves as teacher educators. First, issues of low status have continued to be associated with teacher education, and perhaps identifying with such an area creates problems of low self-esteem. Then it may be that the actual number of teacher educators has decreased as a result of declining student enrollments in the area. And finally, education as a field has greatly expanded within the last 10 years to include many new areas which faculty can identify as their area of program specialization. (p. 224)

Higher education faculty are enigmatic individuals even when members of clearly defined departments such as English or history; given the lack of clear academic boundaries around their field of inquiry and incomplete acceptance by the academy, teacher educators are even more so. For many faculty in other disciplines, education is a study dependent on other disciplines, including sociology and psychology, for its existence. Teacher educators are an ill-defined and poorly understood segment of the higher education faculty population. I once described them as being "among the least welcome guests at the educational lawn party of the establishment of higher education" (Ducharme, 1986a, p. 39). Not only are they among the least welcome, they are also among the most recent guests at this lawn party. Lasley (1986) notes the poor reputation education faculty have had historically.

Education professors are among the most maligned of academics. Their research is often viewed as lacking scholarship, their classes as devoid of substance, and their intellectual focus as too-school-based. Those who hold the title "education professor" putatively are held to a lesser standard than faculty colleagues from the liberal arts departments and professional schools across the campus. These and other (mis)conceptions are often difficult to combat given the realities of academic life. (n.p.)

He goes on to observe that "Rather than trying to be like others in the academic community, perhaps we should acknowledge that our development, indeed our profession's emergence, is dependent on an increased recognition of our unique nature and needs."

For a long time there were few higher education institutions–other than normal schools–employing faculty to prepare teachers in a four-year bachelor's program, a fifth year, or a master's degree program, or any formal teacher preparation programs as we presently know them. These earlier institutions had no supervisors, no methods faculty, no educational historians, no learning theorists, no specialists in pedagogy to guide and assist prospective teachers. Current teacher education faculty may still suffer from this lack of a long tradition on higher education campuses:

> [Education] faculty may still not be "at home" in higher education. It may be that the Janus-like nature of their lives, looking toward both the "field" and academe, produces a schizophrenic quality to their lives, best revealed in our study through interviews. (Ducharme & Agne, 1982, pp. 35–36)

Thus an important problem in this study is the definition of the term *teacher educator*. Faculty from many disciplines are involved in the preparation of teachers. In the past decade, the authors of numerous reports and studies on the lower schools have cited the need for better teachers (Carnegie Forum, 1986; National Commission on Excellence in Education, 1983; Holmes Group, 1986). Some writers of this "reform" literature link the preparation of better, more highly qualified teachers to improvements in the general education that prospective teachers acquire in their undergraduate studies, thus arguing that arts and sciences faculty are teacher educators. While the argument may be both relevant and provocative, the fact of the matter is that these faculty generally do not see themselves as teacher educators even though they do, in a broad sense, educate teachers. Inasmuch as arts and sciences faculty provide the general education for prospective teachers, they are perforce teacher educators. Yet the content, reform, improvement, or change in general education are the responsibilities of arts and sciences faculty, not that of teacher education faculty, even though on some campuses they may work in concert with arts and sciences faculty. Murray and Fallon (1990) present several examples of nascent cooperation between teacher education and arts and sciences faculty with shared responsibility for the education of teachers. For example, they observe that "the University of Northern Colorado, for instance, canceled all classes for half a day so the university could focus on teacher education by forming twelve discipline-based task forces of faculty, students and public school teachers" (p. 21). This example and a few others remain the exceptions, however. Arts and sciences faculty generally do not lay claim to the term *teacher educator* nor wish to be associated with prospective teachers beyond having them in their classes.

When the general public or self-appointed critics of public education perceive the quality of teaching in the lower schools to be either poor or declining, they do not blame the professors in arts and sciences; they blame the education faculty, a situation that arts and sciences faculty are quite content to let rest. Lanier and Little (1986) contend that "it is common knowledge that professors in the arts and sciences risk a loss of academic respect, including promotion and tenure, if they assume clear interest in or responsibility for teacher education" (p. 530). In any event, however important arts and sciences faculty may be to the education of teachers, they are not the teacher educators with whom I am concerned.

In 1986, I defined the term *teacher educator* thus:

> They are those who hold tenure-line or "hard money" positions in schools, colleges, and departments of education [SCDEs], teach beginning and advanced students in professional education, and conduct research or engage in scholarly studies germane to professional education. (Ducharme, 1986a, pp. 43–44)

Carter (1984) had earlier used a similar definition in her one-institution study of teacher educators: "a faculty member in a tenure track position who taught at least one required undergraduate professional education course during the preceding 12 months" (pp. 125–126). Carter's definition is narrow in that it included the condition that they must annually teach undergraduates. I have used the phrasing "beginning and advanced," in order to include all those who are full time, campus-based faculty providing teacher education instruction whether undergraduate, graduate, or inservice.

The number and size of institutions preparing teachers—ranging from very small programs employing as few as three faculty to very large university programs employing more than a hundred faculty–further complicate the problem of definition. The number of institutions that prepare teachers changes somewhat from year to year, but it remains between twelve and thirteen hundred (Clifford & Guthrie, 1988, p. 38). Obviously, what teacher educators do in institutions of such different types and sizes will vary considerably (Goodlad, Soder, & Sirotnik, 1990a), thus making specific definition based on tasks difficult. I once classified teacher educators as follows: "School person, scholar, researcher, methodologist, and visitor to a strange planet" (Ducharme, 1986a, pp. 44–45). I differentiated among each of these by the degrees to which individuals' behaviors were either more like those encountered in the lower schools or more like those encountered in higher education. While hardly empirical, the distinctions are useful.

Although some schools of education offer doctoral degrees specifically in teacher education, they are small in number. Thus individuals who either identify themselves as teacher educators or are identified as teacher educators may have doctoral degrees with concentrations in such areas as mathematics, education, or English education but do the work of teacher educators.

In this study, I was interested only in those working on higher education campuses and ostensibly employed to conduct the work of teacher preparation. In the years since I wrote the definition above, the additional research on the education professoriate and on teacher education faculty that others and I have done and the need for a more appropriate definition have led me to alter it slightly:

> Those who hold tenure-line positions in teacher preparation in higher education institutions, teach beginning and advanced students in teacher education, and conduct research or engage in scholarly studies germane to teacher education.

The substitution of "teacher preparation education in higher education institutions" for "schools, colleges, and departments of education" makes this definition both more restrictive and more useful for analysis than the previous one. Thus the teacher educators in this book are the campus-based faculty who provide professional knowledge and guided field experience for prospective and practicing teachers. They have the major responsibility in the professional preparation and continuing development of America's teachers and are a vital force in the teacher preparation and development process. A better understanding of their roles and responsibilities is critical to the welfare of teacher preparation in all American universities and colleges that offer preparation programs.

REVIEW OF THE LITERATURE

Past Scholarship

In the past, little writing about professors of education resulted from disciplined inquiry; most of it was either descriptive or rhetorical. Hazlett (1989) argues that there is no history of the education professoriate: "A complete accounting of the education professoriate cannot be given. There is no comprehensive study of the origins and development of the education professoriate" (p. 12). There are, however, the beginnings of scholarly inquiry into the lives of education faculty of the past, a process that may produce some of the history that Hazlett claims is missing. For example, in a chapter based on journals, letters, diaries, and other archival materials, Allison (1989) richly describes the lives of three early professors of education at the University of Tennessee. Although descriptive of these individual lives, their stories provide only the beginnings of insight into the totality of the lives of early professors of education who were also teacher educators. Indeed, Allison himself argues that scholars must produce many more such depictions before there will be a full perspective on early education faculty. He also contends that most institutions have archival material that would serve scholars well in writing these studies of early professors of education.

Allison's portraits reveal convincingly the dilemma that has beset teacher education and its faculty from its beginnings: What is the nature of scholarship and research appropriate to the profession? Untrained in the practices of scholarship, Allison's faculty trio conducted surveys and published the results, wrote homiletic essays, published occasional entreaties, and gave seemingly innumerable presentations; in brief, they performed the panoply of largely nonacademic activities of some present-day teacher education faculty, a range of activities that may exacerbate the problem of ownership of teacher education within higher education, even to the present. Who in an academic institution, after all, would want a faculty unit that was not academic? Palmer (1985) describes what may have contributed over the years to the lack of a center of responsibility for teacher education:

> Training programs that were established tended to disappear after a few years. Then, as now, public universities were not certain how to deal with teacher education or if they wanted it. The low status of teacher education in state universities was established early, and it has persisted. (p. 52)

A few writers have described early teacher education programs detailing the development of normal schools in several states, the nature of the curricula, the size of the enrollments, and similar topics. Warren's (1989) *American Teachers: Histories of a Profession at Work* contains excellent chapters on the history of the education of teachers. Borrowman (1956), in his documentary history of teacher education, describes the attempts to develop effective pedagogy in prospective teachers, the struggle for institutional survival, and the development of programs. These authors and a few other education historians provide little about teacher education faculty beyond demographic data, institutional facts and figures, anecdotes about the pedagogy of teacher educators, and occasional comparisons to arts and sciences faculties. In addition to these conventional histories and typical academic studies, there is Koerner's *The Miseducation of American Teachers* (1963), a work in which he finds fault with nearly every aspect of teacher education.

An Example from Fiction

Fiction sometimes informs as much as fact. Robertson Davies (1986), the Canadian novelist, in describing the preparation for teaching one of his characters experienced early in the twentieth century, well captures what early teacher educators did:

> These teachers, it must be explained, were not so much engaged in teaching, as in teaching how to teach. It was their task to impart to the young men and women in their care the latest and most infallible method of cramming information into the heads of children. Recognizing that few teachers have that burning enthusiasm which makes a method of instruction unnecessary, they sought to provide methods which could be depended upon when enthusiasm waned or when it burned out, or when it had never existed. They taught how to teach; they taught when to open the windows in a classroom and when to close them; they taught how much coal and wood it takes to heat a one-room rural school where the teacher is also the fireman; they taught methods of decorating classrooms for Easter, Thanksgiving, Hallo'een and Christmas; they taught ways of teaching children with no talent for drawing how to draw; they taught how a school choir could be formed and trained where there was no instrument but a pitchpipe; they taught how to make a teacher's chair out of a barrel, and they taught how to make hangings, somewhat resembling batik, by drawing in wax crayon on unbleached cotton, and pressing it with a hot iron. They attempted, in fact, to equip their pupils in a year with skills which it had taken them many years of practical teaching, and much poring over Department manuals, to acquire. (Davies, p. 79)

Davies's fictional depiction of early Canadian teacher educators closely resembles the composite that emerges from the limited number of portraits of early American teacher educators as in Allison's work (1989). In fact, some contemporary teacher educators may blush when reading Davies's words because their own work in the 1990s may not be significantly different from that in his description. In any event, the activities in Davies's remarks are part of what teacher educators did and form part of the historical roots of teacher education. The activities themselves, anti-intellectual as they are, may have contributed to the low academic esteem with which faculty in other academic units regard many teacher educators and to which Palmer (1985) and others allude. Teacher education is only now emerging from an apprenticelike model to one based on informed practice and supported by respectable research.

Recent and Emerging Scholarship

A growing number of individuals in the past few years have been conducting a variety of both quantitative and qualitative studies of education faculty. They are providing increasingly specific data on education faculty as well as a growing body of analysis. For example, Howey, Yarger, and Joyce (1978) report that

> The typical teacher educator is a man in his early 40s, though over one-third of his colleagues are women. About half the faculty are full professors, with a third being associate professors, and the rest either assistant professors or lecturers. The great majority of full-time faculty in teacher education are tenured. In many ways, the teacher education faculty member resembles the student described earlier, and why not—many professors have been recruited from that population. About 87 percent of them are white, 8 percent are black, and the rest represent other visible minorities. They tend to come either from a smaller city or rural area, with about 30 percent reporting rural backgrounds. (p. 17)

Judge (1982) in *American Graduate Schools of Education: A View from Abroad* comments on several schools of education in major research universities after he had visited them. One of his major points was the little value that such institutions, their faculties, and their administrations have for teacher preparation. He contends that the more distant education faculty are from teacher education the better they feel about themselves. Ironically, it may be that when education faculty distance themselves from teacher education they most resemble arts and sciences faculty, who, as Lanier and Little (1986) have pointed out, almost totally distance themselves from it. Clifford and Guthrie (1988) in *Ed School*, a detailed study of several schools of education, include extensive remarks about teacher education faculty. In *The Professors of Teaching* Wisniewski and I (1989b) include chapters on the various facets of the education professorial life, with most of the material concerned with teacher educators. Howey and Zimpher (1989), in their study of teacher education programs, *Profiles of Preservice Teacher Education*, comment indirectly on the quality of life of teacher education faculty at the institutions they studied. In editing *Critical Studies in Teacher Education: Its Folklore, Theory and Practice*, Popkewitz (1987) includes various authors presenting their views on the many facets of teacher education in higher education. Numerous articles in journals such as *Journal of Teacher Education, Educational Studies*, and *Phi Delta Kappan* have been devoted to the subject.

Teacher educators have been the focus of the annual surveys (1987–1991) of the RATE Committee of AACTE. These studies, published in annual reports starting in 1987, have provided demographic data on teacher educators, descriptions of their activities, data on their research and scholarship, details on their programs and students; and analyses of the institutions in which they teach. The demographics are remarkably similar to those in Howey, Yarger, and Joyce's (1978) work mentioned previously.

The Society of Professors of Education publishes monographs and occasional papers depicting portions of the picture of the education professoriate, but lacking a comprehensive view. For example, Bagley (1975) edited *The Professor of Education: An Assessment of Conditions*; it contains several thoughtful pieces on the education professoriate but is limited in scope. The society continues to publish monographs and articles adding to the accumulation of scholarly material on the topic.

Clark (1978) provides data on the research and development productivity of education faculty and their institutions as do Agne and I (Ducharme & Agne, 1982). The latter show education faculty as productive in writing as academics generally. Yet despite these materials, Hazlett's (1989) observation of the writing about the education professoriate holds true for the writing about the teacher education professoriate:

> Writings on the professoriate tend to fall into three genres: those that focus on the characteristics of the professoriate, those that seek to define the role, and those that deal with a range of conceptual and/or descriptive matters. (p. 13)

Hazlett contends that writing about the education professoriate must move beyond these levels into history, analysis, and other more substantive genres.

In *Places Where Teachers Are Taught*, one of the three volumes emanating from the Study of the Education of Educators, Goodlad, Soder, and Sirotnik (1990a) have begun what Hazlett contends must be done. Heavily data driven and demographically focused, their work contains important findings about preparation programs, students, sites for student teaching, and higher education institutions. They also provide information and insights on faculty from the 29 institutions in the study. The faculty completed questionnaires dealing with a variety of topics, including faculty perception of institutional mission and their role in it, the process of gaining tenure, the importance of teaching versus research and scholarship. The study also includes numerous quotations from on-site interviews with faculty. Some of the data are similar to those gathered in the annual RATE surveys; scholars could profitably conduct analyses of the material in the two data sources. The three books that have come from the Study of the Education of Educators – *The Moral Dimensions of Teaching* (1990), *Teachers for Our Nation's Schools* (1990), and *Places Where Teachers Are Taught* (1990) – comprise the most comprehensively based and broadly sketched depiction of teacher education to the present time. Yet the picture remains incomplete.

What is needed is an insightful description of faculty lives, their beliefs, and their views of the profession. The series of in-depth interviews I conducted with a number of teacher educators at a variety of institutions and this resultant text will provide some needed insights into teacher educators beyond the merely statistical.

METHODOLOGY OF THE STUDY

The Sample

The experience of the 34 faculty in my sample ranges from that of one female assistant professor in her first year of teaching at a university as a full-time faculty member to a recently retired male full professor and department chair who had been in higher education for 33 years. There are 22 males and 12 females, 17 tenured professors, 10 tenured associate professors, and 7 untenured assistant professors. Although I was not seeking a totally representative sample in the study, those interviewed approximate the percentages in the education professoriate nationally. In Table 1.1, figures from the 1988 RATE study and the United States Department of Education (Russell, Cox, Williamson, Boismier, Javitz, Fairweather, & Zimbler, 1990) are provided for comparison.

The teacher educators I interviewed came from 11 institutions. At

Table 1.1 Study Sample Characteristics Compared to USDE and RATE Faculty Data

Study	Sex (%)		Professorial Rank (%)			
	Male	Female	Full	Associate	Assistant	Other
Ducharme	65	35	50	29	20	0
USDE	62	38	35	29	27	8
RATE	72	28	45	30	20	5

Sources: USDE = Russell et al., 1990; RATE = RATE-III, 1988.

each institution I had a contact person, or informant, who recommended interviewees, and facilitated the interviews. The criteria for recommendation by the informant were that each interviewee must have had full-time teaching experience in the lower schools for a period of more than two years, and be currently a bona fide, full-time, general-fund-supported faculty member working in teacher education. I desired to interview only individuals with previous experience in the lower schools for two reasons: First, individuals with these experiences are seen as more credible by the profession than faculty lacking the experience, and second and more important, such a condition reflects the usual experiences of teacher educators:

> Nearly all teacher education faculty in the RATE study have had prior experience in the lower schools as teachers, department chairs, and administrators, a condition reflected in other studies and writings about the education professoriate (Ducharme & Agne, 1982; Lanier & Little, 1986). Nearly 80% of elementary and secondary faculty had several years of prior work in elementary and secondary schools. (Ducharme & Kluender, 1990, p. 46)

I was also interested in having faculty reflect on the differences between their lives in the lower schools and in higher education. Obviously, only those with experiences in both places could do this reflecting. The reason for limiting the sample to those on full-time, general-fund-supported positions is obvious: anything less and they would not be bona fide members of the professoriate.

The only other "guideline" occurred in institutions in which I would interview more than two faculty. Prior to my visits, I asked the informants to recommend individuals who, in their judgment, represented a range from "star" quality faculty to adequate, without indicating to me which individuals were which. The reason for this qualification was that I desired, where possible, to reflect something of a range of the professoriate without overly structuring the process. I was not interested in establishing cohorts of "good" and "bad" teacher educators, but rather in coming up with a sufficiently large number that would provide the variety that inheres in the teacher education professoriate.

I was personally acquainted with four of the interviewees prior to the study. It also turned out that it was a rare person in the study with whom I did not have some personal connection through a mutual acquaintance or professional experience. I attribute both these conditions to my having been actively involved in the field for so long and to the small world of teacher education with its common rounds of conferences and institutes, commonly read journals, and generally shared culture. Neither my knowing several of the faculty nor my being acquainted with other faculty members' associates appeared to have much effect on the interview responses.

The Institutions

The institutions from which the interviewees were drawn included four private liberal arts colleges, three former state teachers colleges, two of which are not state universities, two private universities, and two "flagship" state universities. All the institutions are in the East, South, and Midwest; all but one are essentially residential institutions with relatively few day students. Another way of defining the institutions is to use the RATE method of arranging institutions into strata: Stratum 1, bachelor's degree only; Stratum 2, bachelor's plus master's degree; Stratum 3, bachelor's, master's, and doctorate. This study has four Stratum 1, two Stratum 2, and five Stratum 3.

One might assume that the range of institutions, from four-year colleges through university would have a wide range of differences in faculty lifestyle, in types of faculty employed, in expectations of the faculty role, in resources available, and in other related areas. The RATE data suggest differences in expectations that faculty have for themselves based on the kinds of institutions in which they work as well as expectations about what the institutions expect of them. In these data, for example, faculty in bachelor's degree institutions have quite different perceptions about the work they do versus what they perceive to be the institutional expectations about their work. Research and scholarship are clearly areas about which there are varied perceptions in the levels of institutions. For example, the RATE faculty in bachelor's level institutions and those in doctoral level institutions report different expectations about the amount of teaching and the value placed on it (Ducharme & Kluender, 1990). The type of institution plays a only minor part in how a few faculty in this study perceive themselves relative to the sacred triad of teaching, research, and service; age, type of preparation, presence or lack of a mentor, and time of entry into the professoriate appear to play at least equally important parts in these perceptions.

The Interview Protocol

Over a period of several months, I developed, pilot tested, and experimented with a series of questions. With only minor variation in the wording, these became the statements and questions used throughout the interviews:

1. Tell me about your introduction to teaching at the lower levels, how you made the decision to teach.
2. What are some of the effects on your current work in higher education of your earlier years in the public schools?
3. How do you think you have changed professionally and personally since becoming a faculty member in higher education?
4. What has been your experience with mentors or other influential individuals at various stages of your career?
5. What were key experiences or programs, in addition to or in lieu of mentors, that influenced you?
6. How do you regard your colleagues within your academic unit with respect to their overall effectiveness as faculty members?
7. What emphasis do administrators (deans or chairs) in your academic unit give to faculty scholarship and research?
8. How does being/not being at a Holmes Group institution affect you?
9. (a) What are the sources of satisfaction in your work? (b) What are the sources of frustration in your work?
10. What is your opinion of the academic ability of students currently enrolled in your institution's professional preparation programs?
11. In terms of your own lifetime of reading of all kinds—personal, professional, or any other kind—what are three books that you would like to have the graduates of your program read before they begin their careers, books that you think would make them better teachers and better people?

The Dilemmas of Interviewing

As we know, when people tell their own stories there is never total reliability. Individuals may often select what they want to say, forget things or choose to omit them for whatever reason, exaggerate what happened, and so forth. Robertson Davies (1983) in his novel *World of Wonders* is to the point:

> It's the classic problem of autobiography; it's inevitably life seen and understood backwards. However honest we try to be in our recollections we cannot help falsifying them in terms of later knowledge, and especially in terms of what we have become. What I can't decide is how much of what we have heard we are to take as fact. It's the inescapable problem of the autobiography: how much is left out, how much has been genuinely forgotten, how much has been touched up to throw the subject into striking relief? (p. 606)

Individuals can never be that which they once were. Certainly, as I interviewed, then listened to the tapes, and finally typed the transcripts, I kept in mind that oftentimes people invent interpretations of the past that correspond with their present view of themselves; they might omit certain portions of their pasts or aggrandize other portions to provide the necessary psychological comfort. The idea in Davies's phrase "of what we had become" was often in my mind for I could not forget that as these faculty talked about their pasts, they were speaking from the perspective of higher education faculty who had left the world of the lower schools and had passed through several phases of adult development. I wondered about the degree to which their positions and their developmental status colored their reminiscences.

These individuals, like all adults, had more than likely undergone fundamental change in their personal development. Once individuals make a developmental shift, it is difficult for them to return to the way they once thought and to understand the past as they lived it at the time; they have become different people, able to interpret those pasts from different, perhaps richer perspectives. In their unique ways, they may have begun to attach meanings to events that were not there for them when the events themselves occurred; they may understand things differently from the way they once did. They cannot be the same persons that they once were. Thus the personae through which they speak as they describe their pasts are both informed and biased. These conditions do not detract from the value of revelations about their pasts; they merely add to the depth of those revelations. They also made me cautious about interpreting their remarks and, perhaps equally important, forced me to guard my own reactions to what I was hearing.

In addition to the developmental phases they have passed through and may be presently in, these individuals are in specific professional developmental phases. A heightened sense of self importance may have accompanied their shifts from being a public school teacher, counselor, or administrator to being a higher education faculty member; at the very least, a different world view has likely emerged. For whatever reasons, *professor* as title has more social prestige than *teacher*. I was curious to see what difference this might have made.

Knowing that they now were carrying the labels of higher education faculty, I wondered if they would talk frankly about their early experiences in the schools or if the prestige of academic titles and university appointments would impede candor. Having completed the interviews and studied the texts carefully, I cannot answer the question of the degree of frankness with which they spoke beyond saying that there was a broad range of admissions about these experiences, from stories of near ineptness to great successes. It would be difficult to imagine what the interview transcripts would look like with more honesty. Were they dissembling somewhat and speaking more for the tape recorder than for honest revelation? Are both the ineptness anecdotes and the success stories but different sides of the persona coin? I do not know; they appeared to be direct and forthcoming, sometimes appearing surprised at what they had said.

I find great appeal in these conversations. The persona one wants to be in a given context emerges. For both the interviewer and the interviewee, there are moments of truth. All of us "know" our past and can cite chapter and verse about past incidents; we may color them differently depending on the circumstances. For example, many males in bull sessions with other males will tell one version of their undergraduate years and the degree to which they were hell-raisers; talking with their teenage sons, they may tell quite another version. Closer to the point, professors telling undergraduate stories of their first year of teaching may describe these experiences quite differently to a visiting professor like myself, with similar experiences, from the way they might describe them to a group of students about to begin their student teaching. In the second instance, the stories may portray the professor as wise young teacher while in the first the role may be that of the earnest young professional doing all the right things in a crass world; or the stories may be reversed. The point is we simply do not know the degree of verisimilitude we are getting.

Conducting the Interviews

I conducted all interviews except two on the campus of the professors; the lone exceptions being those with a retired faculty member and a faculty member at a conference. Both of these were conducted in restaurants. I interviewed most of the faculty in their own offices; in two instances, a special room had been set up for conducting the interviews. In general, the faculty interviewed in their offices appeared relaxed. The two I interviewed in a designated room appeared tense, and in both instances I immediately requested that I be allowed to conduct the remainder of those interviews in faculty offices. I received immediate approval in both instances with the apologetic observation that a special room had been originally set aside for my convenience and to be helpful.

All interviewees responded to the set of questions above, with minor variations on the wording as indicated. Interviews lasted from 40 to 65 minutes. I audiotaped and subsequently transcribed all interviews. During each interview, after a few moments of "warm-up" conversation, I asked my first question and the interviewee responded until he or she felt a sense of closure on the topic. Occasionally, when the interviewee appeared to be going too far afield in one response, I moved the conversation on to the next question, but generally I allowed full reign to the respondents. Each interview was followed by some exchanges about the experience of being interviewed. Interviewees often said they had never previously thought of the things discussed in quite the manner that had just occurred. They frequently expressed surprise that they had remembered something in the interview that they had not thought of in a quite a while.

The interviewer may sometimes be nearly as important as the interviewee. Much may depend on the interviewer's abilities to establish rapport, create a feeling of trust and intimacy, suspend judgment, occasionally elicit additional information, and be a good listener. In my work during the past 25 years, I have conducted many interviews as part of commissioned studies, program reviews, follow-up assessments, and numerous other activities requiring a high order of interview skills. Glesne and Peshkin (1992) effectively present the complexities of interviewing,

> Interviewing is a complex act. We say this to produce not faint hearts but, rather, realistic users who will be fair to themselves especially in the nervous early days of interviewing when it might be easier to conclude, "This is not for me" than to exult "What a wonder I am." Interviewing is complex because of the number of things that are happening simultaneously. Because there are so many acts to orchestrate, effective interviewing should be viewed the way that good teaching is: you should look for improvement over time, for continuing growth, rather than for mastery or perfection. (p. 76)

Most interviewees had little idea why I was there prior to my sitting down and providing a brief introduction to my study, beyond knowing that someone had asked them if they would be willing to talk with a professor on sabbatical who was studying the work of professors of teacher education. Two or three indicated that they had given some thought to what they might say while driving to work the morning of the interview, even though they admitted they didn't know what I was going to ask them. In a couple of instances, when I remained in one institution for several days, individuals scheduled for interview on the last day chatted with faculty I had interviewed on the first or second day and thus had some sense of what I was going to ask them to talk about.

As many individuals who have conducted interviews will attest, most people enjoy talking about themselves. The questions in the protocol invited interviewees to talk about themselves. As the faculty talked about the successes and failures in their professional lives, they were no different from the rest of the world. They, too, at one level, are the cynosures of their existence and welcome the opportunity to talk about themselves. Generally, no more than a couple of minutes elapsed before the individual would begin to speak at length in an apparently unreserved manner. Words, phrases, and sentences would gush forth; one recollection would evoke another. Occasionally I probed a bit when something appeared to me to be of unusual interest. Usually, however, I needed little probing beyond asking the opening question, which, no matter how worded, clearly meant "Tell me about yourself and your work."

Although they may be the unwelcome guests at someone else's lawn party, as the quotation cited earlier suggests about some teacher educators, these faculty generally gave evidence of feeling very much at home in higher education; they did not feel or did not express the idea that they were in a strange place. Despite including descriptions of difficult times and occasional discomfort with the "new" norms of higher education, they affirmed their experiences and existence through their stories. Some higher-education institutions may not be ready for some teacher educators, but many of these teacher educators are very much ready for and involved in higher education and think it the place they should be. Where are they in the academic firmament? Secure? Anxious? Confident? Perhaps a little of each. In subsequent chapters, readers will be able to make decisions on this matter by reading the words of the faculty themselves. Certainly the faculty will be more comprehensively described and, it is hoped, better understood.

This text provides a look at the lives of teacher educators in their own words, complemented by my interpretive observations, and occasionally supplemented by references to the teacher education literature. Although in no way comprehensive about all teacher educators in all situations, the 34 interviews provide a series of rich observations and perceptions from the point of view of the people doing the work.

2 Beginning to Teach

You know, the draft was on, and I didn't know what to do. And this chance to teach came along, so I did it.

—Male professor

In this chapter I delineate the reasons that teacher education faculty gave for their initial choice to teach and describe some of the influences informing that choice. I then describe some of their early experiences in teaching in the lower schools, experiences which, as I will show in Chapter 3, had major effects on their subsequent professional lives.

The literature on teachers in the lower schools reveals that they often choose teaching as a career somewhat causally, almost accidentally. When asked for specific reasons why they entered teaching, teachers usually cite one or more of several reasons, some idealistic, others pragmatic. Lortie (1975) postulated what he called "five attractors to teaching" (p. 30). They include:

1. The interpersonal theme or the fondness for working with people
2. The service theme or the performing of a special service for society
3. The continuation theme or the "staying in school" opportunity
4. The material benefits theme or things such as job security
5. The theme of time compatibility or the vacations and shorter on-the-job hours aspects of teaching

All the individuals interviewed in this study had teaching experience in the lower schools prior to doctoral studies and subsequent appointment to teacher education faculty roles in higher education, roles which most of them had consciously sought. Because they had successfully completed the transitions from lower-school teacher to doctoral student to higher education faculty member, a process that would seemingly require planning and sense of purpose, I wondered if these 34 experienced teacher educators might have been more systematic in their original choice to teach than lower school teachers generally are. Perhaps they might have even considered several career options and chosen teaching for carefully determined reasons. Such was not the case. In general, their reasons for initially selecting teaching as a career were no more sophisticated or complex than those of the teachers in Lortie's study or of those in others' studies, such as Spencer's (1986).

REASONS FOR ENTERING TEACHING

I asked them to respond to the following statement: "Tell me about your introduction to teaching at the lower levels, how you made the decision to teach." A careful reading of their responses reveals, perhaps not surprisingly, that they turned out to be much like most teachers, making their choices for the same kinds of reasons or lack of reasons.

Chance

The most common factor for faculty, particularly males, was chance; variously called accident, fate, or some other external, uncontrollable source cited. Some appeared proud at not having deliberately "chosen" a teaching career, as though there is more dignity to accidentally entering a not too highly regarded career.

A male senior educational foundations faculty member at a state university saw "accident" as the prime mover in his decision to teach in the lower schools:

> By accident, by accident. I was in ROTC. For a lot of programmatic reasons I was delayed going into active duty following my commission. I had a year of hanging around. With Franco–American parents, you don't hang around for a year doing nothing. I was about to accept a position being a credit manager for a furniture company when my brother who was a teacher called and said they needed substitutes. He was in some program at the junior high and said they needed subs at the high school.

Thus began a career from potential credit manager by default to secondary school teacher to ultimately becoming a distinguished, widely published faculty member at a state university. His "choice" was the result of a telephone call from his brother at a moment when he was unemployed and at time of relaxed certification practices because of teacher shortages. As he subsequently observed, he was able to obtain the position because of an emergency situation during which uncertified people could teach.

> At first they said no because I'd had no education courses–that's strange because the whole rest of my career I've been in defense of professional courses–but they had these classes called "streamer classes" which no one else wanted and they let me teach them. So I taught for a year and then went in the military, came back and taught some more.

Thus a career begun through chance, temporary availability, and relaxed standards of entry.

For another, the "choice" came about because of experiences acquired as a result of his being drafted into military service immediately after graduating from college. This individual, now a retired social studies educator and university chair, discovered his interest in teaching while in the United States Army during World War II.

> I was involved in a lot of teaching in the Army. I was very impressed with the teaching at Fort Benning; they were using a lot of visual aids, stuff that I had never seen in my education. I was in the infantry and you know in the infantry you do only one of two things, you either fight or you train. So I became a trainer. And I decided that when I got home out of the army that I would go into teaching.

He went on to say that he did very little thinking about it beyond that quick decision. A graduate of Harvard College without teacher certification, he obtained a teaching position in a small country day school in the Northeast, a position he abandoned after two years because he thought he did not know anything about teaching or the young people whom he was teaching. The turbulence disturbed him, "I was teaching sixth through ninth grade and singly unsuccessful with the junior high-school level, particularly the eighth-grade kids, all the turbulence, the volatility. They were little crops of mercury scooting all over the place." He was faced with the challenges to authority that Sikes, Measor, and Woods (1985) state confront nearly all teachers early in their careers. "At some time during their first year, teachers often experience 'critical incidents' to do with discipline. Frequently these incidents take the form of a challenge to their authority, and thereby their professional identity" (p. 29). He thereupon sought a master's degree in education, followed by a few years of successful teaching of social studies in the secondary schools, a master's degree in history, a Ph.D. in education, and a 20-year career at a major school of education. But it all began through the accidents of classification and assignment in the United States Army.

Another male professor was affected by the military and the times during which he lived:

> Went to undergraduate school, Hobart. I wasn't really sure what I wanted to do. I did take a couple of basic education courses, but I couldn't major in education. I did think I wanted to go into teaching. I got drafted during the Korean War and was discharged. I'd decided during the time I had in the service to teach when I got out. That was the time New York had the Intensive Teacher Training Program. There was a real shortage of teachers. So I went into that program at Cortland, got my first teaching job up in the Adirondacks, in a junior high.

For him, the time in the service was an opportunity to reflect on what he might do with his life. While he had taken "a couple of basic education courses" in college, he indicated that he was not at all certain that teaching is what he would have done had he not been in the military.

Going into military service was critical for some, but staying out of the military provided an opportunity for another male, an associate professor of special education, who did not want to go to Vietnam:

> I graduated from high school in 1968, and I wanted to avoid going to Southeast Asia, so I continued with my education. [I was] a psychology major at first, [and] even though I ended up majoring in English, it was easy to get into special education. Actually after a few practicum experiences – serendipitous – it became apparent that I was also interested in working with the severely handicapped. I should have been able to get a job in the summer with the state highway department, [but] that didn't work out, and I ended up working in a development center. So I ended up getting paid while I was going to school. When I got out of school that same development center offered me a teaching job. My job was to teach reading to individuals who were cognitively okay but who had problems. They were very bright and had no business being institutionalized.

Thus chance, represented in part by the military, played a major role in the initial decisions of these men to teach, one through not being taken into the Army when he anticipated he would be, two others going into the service and entering teaching upon their discharges, and a fourth when he was avoiding military service by staying in college. One wonders if there is a present counterpart to the role the military played then, namely, an opportunity to reflect on what to do with one's life while temporarily having something to do that was not quite the beginning of a career. Perhaps the time some recent graduates take to "find themselves" comes the closest.

Limited Options

The recent emphasis on freedom in career choice for more individuals and the ever-increasing range of career possibilities may have blinded us to the fact that there have always been relatively few career opportunities for some segments of the American population, or at least some individuals have perceived that there were relatively few. Some women faculty members, for example, claimed that they chose from few alternatives, that because they were women they were automatically consigned to traditional women's work: teaching, nursing, or working in an office. One woman appeared to have always been a teacher, to have lived her life for a long time in ways that reflect traditionally female teacher patterns. She began it at an early age, was interrupted by undergraduate years, and then marriage. But she was always interested in teaching:

> You mean when I was real young? I've always been interested in teaching. Well, believe it or not, when I was in the eleventh grade I taught a course in continuing education in cake decorating. I taught three or four of those classes for a couple of years. I don't decorate cakes anymore, though. You eat too many of your mistakes when you make cakes.

The 12 women in this study are different from those in Spencer's *Contemporary Women Teachers* (1986), many of whom were as indecisive and unfocused in their choice to teach as the men in this study. Spencer observes of many of her subjects that they "simply 'fell' into it, had no other choice, or did not know why they chose teaching" (p. 169). Of course, Spencer's subjects were still in the lower schools when interviewed while the women in this study have all earned doctorates and taken positions in higher education. A similarity between the women in both groups is that most of them had few choices or alternatives for careers. Spencer noted,

> Those who said they thought there were no other choices apparently chose teaching by default. They knew women could also be secretaries or nurses

but commented that they did not want to sit at a desk all day or could not stand the sight of blood. Eleanor, a 32-year-old, married, elementary school teacher with no children, commented, "My mother always told me, 'Go to school, get a job in case you have to support yourself. A teacher would be good, or a nurse.' I noticed that no one ever recommended that I be a brain surgeon in case I had to support myself." (p. 169)

The women in this study had similar feelings. One senior faculty member spoke of the limitations of her working-class background and the limited options available at that time for women who wanted careers:

> I came from a working-class background, lived on the wrong side of the tracks . . . with the possibility of only two jobs, teaching or nursing. I didn't like blood so I couldn't be a nurse; I might as well be a teacher. I decided I would be a teacher because teachers were wonderful people and I never even thought about doing anything else. But then, I really didn't feel that I had an option.

The choice of teaching over nursing, however hyperbolic the description of the choice may appear in retrospect, made because of a distaste of blood (note the common dislike of blood in the quotation from Spencer above) nicely states the limited options at the time. Three of the 12 women mentioned the nursing-teaching career alternatives; they were all from the tenured full or associate professor ranks and had been in teaching for over twenty years. In their own ways, each expressed a point of view like that expressed by one of the characters in May Sarton's novel *The Small Room*: "Is there a life more riddled with self-doubt than that of a woman professor, I wonder?" (1961).

Of course, while I have included the choices of some of the women under the "Limited Options" heading, I might have equally considered them under "Chance," if one considers a person's gender the result of chance. For, although a higher percentage of the women interviewed indicated an earlier choice for teaching than did most of the males, this choice may have merely been the result of their having been born female.

Another woman, a full professor and department chairperson at a major university, originally thought about science as a career but quickly shifted to teaching when she "learned" that she was not the "type" to become a scientist:

> I started out wanting to be a scientist. It didn't take me long to decide that I wouldn't be very good, that I wasn't the kind of

person to work in laboratories, hours and hours of sitting with those microscopes. I considered myself a people person. I was going to the local teachers college anyway. I stayed there the whole four years and got my degree in science and social studies. I graduated in January and I started substituting at the high school. Then I decided that I really wanted to teach elementary school, so I went back to get my certification in elementary. I taught a few years, and the next to the last year I was in the elementary school I started doing some special ed work.

This woman experienced at least three career alignments because of gender matters, a topic to be covered more fully in Chapters 5 and 6. In sum, however, she shifted her interest from science because of its then heavy "maleness" in addition to her first stated reason of being a "people person"; later male educational administration professors counseled her out of seeking a position in public school administration even though she had obtained a master's in educational administration. "My adviser advised me that might not be a wise thing for a woman to do, that there might not be a lot of opportunities." She took only one "straight" graduate history course during her doctoral study in social studies education because of the patronizing experience she had in the course during which she, the only woman in the course, was often asked for the "distaff" view on matters. The professor also put an extra item on one of the exams, "Something like, 'Who's the ray of sunshine in this class?'" Thus, although she made her choice to be a teacher early in life, this first "choice" and subsequent ones were hindered by the constraints of gender and custom.

None of the five untenured, more recently appointed women faculty mentioned being limited to two choices, perhaps underscoring the fact that educated women are presently maturing with a much broader conception of what they can do with their lives besides teach or nurse.

Meager Resources

Although nearly all of the women in their forties and early fifties expressed the view that there were few options open to them when they began their careers, several men in similar age brackets and from lower socioeconomic backgrounds expressed the same view of limited alternatives open to them. Their responses run counter to the broadly perceived notion that males generally have a larger range of career options open to them than do females. The responses also suggest that limited career choices may have been, in addition to being gender driven, partly a result of social and economic class. It is commonly accepted that many teachers in the public schools have come from the lower and lower-middle social classes (Lanier & Little, 1986; Lortie, 1975) and that for them teaching was a step up the social scale. Few have commented, however, on the possibility that for reasons of social and economic class both men and women may not have seen other options as viable possibilities for them. For example, a male senior foundations professor observed:

> I really wanted to go to the arts center in Los Angeles and be an "artsy" photographer. My parents simply couldn't afford it, so I went to the State University. A dumb kid, 18, and I had all these visions of wonderful things to do. So I took my first book [class text] to social science class and thought that I wanted to be a diplomat, and go into the foreign service. Took a couple of semesters of French. I was going to have some real damn problems with that. But I did like history a lot. I took all the history and political science that they would let me take my first couple of years. I think I was really more interested in doing something with that at the beginning than I was in teaching. I think I entered teaching because I didn't know what else to do. I didn't know what the alternatives were. Or at least for me.

The combination of low economic status and lack of knowledge of what college entailed were clear limiting factors in his choice to become a teacher.

One man expressed a similar limit of two possibilities of careers with teaching being chosen as perhaps the less offensive of the two:

> Frankly, I didn't know there was anything I could be other than a teacher or a farmer, and I didn't want to go to college. I had about three years of credit. I had signed a professional baseball contract. I went to that and broke an arm at the end of the season; that caught me up short. I went home to southern Illinois and this was in 1951 during the Korean conflict. They were desperate for teachers and wanted me to take the exam and teach in a one-room school, that wonderful institution. That's the way I got into teaching.

For another male, a full professor of mathematics education at a major private university, the choice lay between teaching and the ministry. "Well, I came from a family that was professional; my father was a minister. It was expected of me that I would be going into a profession; the ministry did not appeal to me. So I chose teaching out of a desire; well, I hope it was out of a desire to improve schools."

Thus the traditions of work accorded to women—secretarial, nursing, and teaching—had a strong impact on the choices they made. The experiences of several of these male professors in the study, however, suggest that sometimes men perceived equally limited opportunities. The limitations for males, however, were more likely the result of their own lack of vision of what was possible rather than what the women faced: real or imagined social prohibition against careers other than those prescribed as acceptable for them.

Most of the faculty interviewed came from modest or poor backgrounds, a situation echoing Fuller and Bown's (1975) observations about teacher educators, "Teacher educators have, by and large, humble social-class origins and low status in comparison with their academic colleagues" (p. 29). Agne and I concluded similarly:

> SCDE faculty behavior is greatly influenced by their personal and professional backgrounds. These backgrounds generally include: lower-middle and middle-class origins, attendance at nonelitist colleges; lack of family experience in higher education; work in the lower schools; part-time study at both the master's and doctorate levels; and pragmatic dissertations or doctoral projects. . . . Sixty-eight percent of the fathers of professors in our study held positions for which a college education was not the norm, for example, farming. In fact, only 12.6% graduated from college, a low percentage of individuals holding college degrees in the home environment. (Ducharme & Agne, 1989, pp. 68–70)

The perceived lack of choice by males and females underscores the interrelatedness between social and economic origins and career choices in the lives of education faculty that some writers have pointed out (Lanier & Little, 1986; Ducharme & Agne, 1982). In this way, teacher educators, of course, reflect the backgrounds of the teaching force from which they come (Lortie, 1975).

A male full professor, in his early fifties, spoke of the need for job security, a variation on the "material benefits" to which Lortie referred. From a working-class background, this individual had entered college enamored with the idea of being a sports broadcaster, a possibility that reality quickly cured:

> It's probably a typical story; I came out of high school in a small
> town in Pennsylvania in 1957. Because of some experiences where I
> broadcast some basketball games in high school, I decided that I was
> going to be a sports broadcaster. I went to Penn State because of a

good speech program there. After a semester I discovered there were a lot of very poor disk jockeys and announcers and decided that I ought to do something secure. Everybody told me that the pay wasn't good in education, but that you could always get a job, so I decided to get certification. My major was history and after a semester of straddling the fence decided to forget being a sports broadcaster and be a teacher. So I actually went into teaching because it was secure and you could get a job. While I was teaching in the junior high school I had very little social interaction with colleagues. I lived 30 miles from the school and car-pooled with a government worker. We alternated driving and we had four passengers who paid to ride with us.

Like many young men of his time, he married early and soon found that while the teaching job was secure, the need for more income was clear. Driving paying passengers to school in his car was only one way to survive economically. Part-time work became the norm; time became scarce. "I think my time in the schools can be described as scrambling. I was a clerk in a drug store, moonlighting for extra money. So I really didn't do much. I'd get home from school, have fifteen minutes to eat before I went to the drug store." This man's introductory years in teaching illustrate the point that while teaching may be demanding and taxing, one could also hold a part-time job while doing it. Teaching, for him, did not require his full attention. Family economics demanded that he work part time. Sizer's (1984) English teacher in *Horace's Compromise* spends his entire career divided between teaching and a family business.

This faculty member's choice of where to teach, however, indicated his interest in doing something significant and challenging as much as it reflected a need for employment:

I went into junior high school teaching. An urban, inner-city school. I did it for a weird reason. I had student taught in a suburban school which was close to where I lived. One of my professors told me that this junior high school [the urban school] was one of the two most difficult junior high schools to teach in Pennsylvania. My student teacher supervisor's wife taught there. I wanted to try it and see what I could do in that environment. I loved it; and I succeeded.

His remarks reflect a degree of idealism and a sense of obligation to the young, characteristics fairly common among this group of faculty as they talked of their first years in teaching.

An impending marriage and the need to make a living motivated another male whose first choice was to be an engineer:

> I had never thought about going to college until my friends started going to college. I was in a Mennonite community in Kansas. I went to college; I was a math major and I liked science. I had real intentions to be an engineer. To be an engineer, I'd have had to go away; problem was I had met my wife who was in nurse's training and I wanted to get married. I didn't have much of an option. If I wanted to get married I had to find a livelihood. So I picked up and went into teaching.

So he married, became a junior high science teacher in a ghetto school, and started a career far removed from engineering.

Another male professor observed, "When I was very young, it was the end of the Depression. While we didn't have real poverty, we were poor. So any time somebody came along with 25 bucks and said, 'help us with our reading program,' or 50 bucks to 'write us a story,' I did it." He went on to observe that teaching offered a sure income from a regular job that could be relied on. His response echoes Lortie's (1975) contention that the theme of material benefits is a critical variable in career choice for many teachers. Certainly, many of the children of the Great Depression sought jobs that would provide at least minimal economic security; teachers were no exception (Terkel, 1970).

Ease of Entry

Many schools and colleges have for decades offered quick, relatively easy certification programs for liberal arts students who might wish, for whatever reason, to "pick up" teacher certification in the event that other career possibilities do not develop. Many teaching careers have been spawned in the decision to enroll in such programs.

For one woman, it was the familiar story of picking up certification along the way. It was available, why not do it? But student teaching actually captured her interest:

> When I went to undergraduate school, I did not intend to be a teacher or go into education at all. First, I was going to be an English major, then a math major, then ended up a science major after I took freshman biology. Went to a small liberal arts school, about 1,000 students for four years. I needed to teach for only one quarter and [take] three classes to become certified

as a teacher in addition to my biology degree. So I said why not?
Two quarters out of four years and I would have teaching to fall
back on. I loved student teaching. It was the only quarter I had
ever had in my life when I didn't mind getting up in the morning. Thoroughly enjoyed student teaching. And I decided to
be a teacher.

A male faculty member, now a tenured associate professor at a state
university, also started to go someplace else and then honed in on teaching
as what he wanted to do:

I began thinking I was going to be a chemical engineer. When I
was in high school, I had a lot of math, a lot of science. I thought
if I could put those two things together I could be a chemical
engineer. But the fact of the matter was I was not that good a
mathematician or scientist. When I got into undergraduate preparation for engineers, I realized that it wasn't for me, not what
I wanted to spend my life doing. It just didn't feel comfortable.
So for whatever the reasons I decided to spend my life in schools.
It was no more scientific than that. I had a good feeling about
what I was sensing. I was probably better at language usage than at
science or math, probably should have been an English teacher.
As it turns out I majored in biology but taught math because that
was what was needed. I had a very strong minor in math from
the pre-chemical engineering stuff and all I needed was a methods
course and I was certified. I taught there [Ohio] three and a half
years.

Thus, for this individual, early interest waned upon actual acquaintance
with what was involved in the planned career; and teaching with its ease
of access became the replacement career. Another male spoke of the easy
opportunity to become a teacher.

I was raised in upstate New York in a little town that had a state
teachers college. I wanted to go to college and as the time ap-
proached it looked as if I wouldn't be able to go anywhere else.
I went there and loved it. I decided I'd think about teaching,
just think about it. Well, in our junior year we had two 10-week
sessions in the schools and I learned two things: one, I learned
that teachers were pretty human if you encountered them out-
side their classrooms and, two, I learned that I liked teaching.
I liked it and I was good at it; both of those things were sur-

prises. At that point in time, after student teaching, I decided to think seriously about teaching. Up to that time, I was not considering it seriously.

It is interesting to observe that while several of the 34 interviewees spoke of student teaching, none referred to it as the critical phase of their preparation program, where they put theory to practice, where the "real" world of the schools is in conflict with the theory world of the university, or any of the other bromides about student teaching that appear in the literature. Rather, when they talked about student teaching, they described how this experience opened up for them what teaching might be with no reference to the cleavage between theory and practice or to "Ivory Towered" higher education. While one might postulate that this is the case because these faculty now make their living in the academy, the texts of the interviews generally reveal nothing in the way of the higher relevancy of either the academy or of the schools. Rather, there is a consistency in statements about the importance of both.

Model of Other Teachers

Several spoke of teachers who had influenced them in various ways, and some referred directly to a specific teacher as the direct influence of their choice of teaching as a career. One who did so was a male science educator:

Well, I had a music teacher in high school. I was in the band and chorus. She really made me think about being a teacher; she was such a good teacher. But it's hard to separate out when I stopped thinking about being a teacher because of other teachers who'd influenced me and because I just wanted to be a teacher. I guess probably while I was in college.

Another male faculty member, now a professor and director of student teaching at a major university, was greatly influenced in his choice to teach by a science teacher, but he needed a little time and a push from his spouse to make the final decision:

I became interested in education when I was a sophomore in college. I took several courses from a very fine biology teacher and I wasn't too much interested in teaching. I was more interested in the content than I was in the process of teaching. He was such a dynamic teacher that I gave it some thought and finally decided to

give secondary biology teaching a try and went ahead and finished
at the University of Arkansas in secondary science education. I realized that there was very little money in it. . . . I went on the road
for a wholesale paper house for four years. But it got so that every
time I passed a school I knew that I was in the wrong place. I had
trained to become a science teacher; it was time to bite the bullet and
start teaching. I told my wife and her remark was, "I wondered how
long it was going to take you to getting around to making this decision."

Of course, that he was able to work four years at a different kind of job,
take no additional courses, and immediately enter teaching reflects the
ease of entry to teaching that Lortie (1975) and other writers have pointed
out.

For a formal social-studies educator, now a dean of education, it was
the whole range of teachers and their effect on him that made him want
to be a teacher. Coming from immigrant parents and low socioeconomic
background, he found schooling a compelling environment: teachers were
powerful people. He wanted to be like them.

And the decision to become a teacher I think came about in two
ways: one conscious–the other unconscious. The unconscious one
was I had always done well in school–I liked teachers, I was afraid
of them but they were very important people. They were authority
figures and so on. I wanted to please them and I was afraid of
their displeasure. But the conscious part of it was we were all in the
twelfth grade and somebody from the [local] University–the only
university that I knew existed because it was in the city–the admissions person in those days came to talk at a career forum. I asked
my best buddy: "What are you going to do?" He said: "I'm going
to be a teacher." I figured that's all right with me so I put down
that I was going to be a teacher. And I really think it happened that
way.

While he admired teachers, he did not decide to join their ranks on a very
rational basis.

Finally, there was that individual that so many writers have speculated
on, the one who becomes a teacher because of having had a very poor
teacher for a particular subject that he happened to like. He knew he
could do better and felt motivated to right for others the wrong that had
been done to him.

> I went to the state college to major in education so that I could
> be a teacher. Back in high school I had a poor science teacher
> who did a poor job of teaching; I wanted to do a better job of
> teaching than he did. So I went and got a degree in chemistry and
> had a lot of pressure to go the straight science route, but I got a mas-
> ter's degree and picked up the education credits. I went out and
> taught.

Did he do well? He did so well that someone from the university came
and told him that he should do doctoral work so that he could "prepare
teachers at the university"!

Family Influence

It is generally acknowledged that family background with respect to
income, social status, and support plays a part in many people's upbringing
and the emergence of their views. Only one person, however, a woman
special-education faculty member, spoke directly of her family's influence
on her decision to teach, in her case, her father's:

> I really decided I wanted to be a teacher when I was about eight years
> old; my father actually may have been the motivator. He stopped
> school when he was in the eighth grade. Very bright but he was al-
> ways thwarted because of his lack of education. He always told us
> that education is the most important thing you'll ever do. He be-
> lieved that teachers were so important. So to me it's more important
> than having money, than having friends, than anything else. I guess
> that's why I wanted to teach as well. I got a state teachers college
> scholarship. My parents were very poor and could not have afforded
> to send me to school. At that time this state gave teachers scholar-
> ships if you'd agree to teach a number of years in the state. It enabled
> me to go to college.

This woman's story illustrates how a parent can influence one to pursue
education even while knowing little about what "being educated" involves.
The statement that "education is the most important thing you'll ever do"
is strong on exhortation and short on specificity.

Educational levels, social class, and economic status of families may
have had much to do with the lack of advising and prodding to enter
teaching that these faculty received from family members. It is difficult to
advise when one knows little of the situation and is vaguely hoping

that one's children will have lives of a different order from one's own. Agne and I argued that education faculty had limited advice about higher education.

> Given the lack of college backgrounds in the families of future SCDE faculty members, they very likely had little family or home preparation for college. Arguments on behalf of college matriculation may have been made, but there could not have been much experiential conviction for this view in the majority of cases. Chances are good that the arguments came from a belief in education in a general sense, a hope that education might lead to a better life, to more income, to higher social status. But there was little likelihood of much advice on how to survive freshman composition, which professors to choose, which dorm to select, or fraternity or sorority to join. (Ducharme & Agne, 1989, p. 71)

This woman's story typifies those of many who went from meager family educational backgrounds to become the first to attend college; guidance is difficult beyond vague urgings to improve oneself.

EARLY EXPERIENCES

Difficult Moments

While these faculty regarded their lower school teaching experience as invaluable, life in the schools had its difficult moments. In their initial experiences, some of these individuals were not at all unlike those student teachers and beginning teachers some of them now supervise and work with. They received the "bad" teaching assignments as first-year teachers, had discipline problems, found the work tiring and demanding, lacked assuredness about what they were doing. One person was in fear of losing his job: "I finally realized after three years that I wasn't doing very well; in fact, I was about to get fired."

Two females, one who started out as a special educator and one who started as a regular teacher, were given nothing but the problem students:

> What they did was cull all these little kids – 12 little kids – out of the kindergarten and first grade classes that they couldn't understand or manage. They put us in a church on a hill 'Get these kids out of here.' You look like a good one – you teach these kids . . . first year of teaching. Twelve kids in a church basement. It was a zoo. It was fun.

The second teacher spoke of survival as a theme of her first year of teaching:

> I had a real rich base: I taught in an army school for my student teaching. My first experience in teaching was on a stage where they had to make a second grade because they had too many second graders for the teachers they had. . . . So each teacher took her five worst kids and they made a class for my first teaching experience from everybody's worst five students. Just to survive that first year was unbelievable.

Although schools often assign first-year teachers to the lower level classes, it is probably rare that a first-year teacher gets a class drawn from the most difficult students at a given grade level. Little wonder that several years later, the second teacher says of her experience: "I draw on it all the time."

Women were not the only ones getting their first students from the worst that a school had to offer. A male professor observed of his first students:

> They had these kids who weren't supposed to graduate. In this class they had thrown the teacher out bodily at the beginning of the year. So I did that for a year. It was fantastic and terrifying. Then the next year, the way the system worked, I was doing so well with these kids that they wanted to move me up to teach the college prep kids.

The last sentence in the previous quotation reveals again the range of experience that these faculty had prior to their higher education experience. In this case, the individual had experienced not only the difficulty of being given the most challenging students to teach but also the process whereby these who "pass" this first arduous test are moved to what are perceived as more benign settings. One cannot help noting that, even years later, he had retained something of the school's way of viewing the world inasmuch as he himself said that "they wanted to move me up to teach the college prep kids." Another individual substituted in the middle of the year: "Then they asked me to substitute for a teacher who'd had a nervous breakdown. I learned a *lot*!"

For these and other faculty in the study, their time in the lower schools was one of challenge and learning. Some got the typical first-year assignments that teachers often receive; some had painful inductions into teaching. All spoke of their early experiences, regardless of the positive or negative aspects to them, with warmth, as things that enriched their lives and provided a context for the next steps of their careers. Such remarks as an exclamation of wonder over being put in the basement of a church with the "worst" kids the school could find or being placed on the stage of the school auditorium, although uttered with much excitement, were not stated with resentment or latent anger. There is no question that these early experiences were vital in the lives of these faculty and contributed to their present career status, one of the subjects of Chapter 3.

Joy and a Sense of Satisfaction

These professors, as with most of those interviewed, expressed considerable pleasure at their decisions to become teachers. Most loved it. "It's [teaching] probably the most important thing that I ever did . . . I loved teaching. I was never very age specific; it didn't matter to me what age I taught. Whatever they asked me to do, I did it, and I loved it."

Another observed, "I enjoyed the public school teaching. I really did. I get really upset when I send out student teachers and some of the teachers out in the school say to them, 'Why is a great person like you going into teaching?'" A director of student teaching with seventeen years of experience in the job said of his present feelings about his former high-school teaching days, "I liked teaching. I loved it. God, the days have never been so short. If I could have the salary that I have now and walk out of here and take up five classrooms of biology—five sections of biology—I'd never look back. Never. Never." He also affirmed that he found fulfillment in his present position: "I want to be known as having helped prepare teachers."

He was not the only one to look back on those early experiences in the lower schools with nostalgia; a senior foundations professor also remembered them with warmth:

> I sense, Ed, that what I experienced in high school teaching was
> a lot more unique than what I have experienced in higher educa-
> tion. . . . It was a real strong community, even though it was in a
> suburban high school. We "palled" around together; we had cook-
> outs probably once a month, two or three couples in a group. We
> were best friends. Friday night poker players, Sunday afternoon
> bridge groups. It was really very close. I suspect that it was probably
> not typical. We still correspond with several of them. Everyone of
> them except two—there were six, seven, or eight over time, some
> came and went—are in higher education, got the doctorate, and went

on. The head of the department became city coordinator of social studies and I think maybe two remained and retired as social studies teachers. It was really a unique group.

Yet another professor observed, "I occasionally get this nostalgic feeling that it would be fun to be in a classroom teaching 25 kids again." For another male faculty member it was a time of pleasure and learning,

> I learned a lot of things. It helped me to understand kids with a wide range of variability; it really did. I had kids in that science thing, kids I never thought would go on to college; they went on to college and did science. I definitely learned a lot from the experience.

Nothing in his interview or in those of the others suggested that they ever looked back on the decision to teach as a lost opportunity to do something else. Thus while the variety of career possibilities open to these faculty may have been few, the one available proved joyful, proved to be an opportunity to earn one's livelihood, but more importantly, to make a contribution to society through working with its young people. It is apparent that none would change the past, a past that still provides meaning for them in their present careers.

CONCLUSION

There is overlap in the headings I have used for the various "reasons" and nonreasons these faculty stated for entering teaching, a perhaps inevitable situation in a career field in which the ease of entry is so evident.

The chanciness of it all, the seeming randomness of career choice is a fact of many of these faculty members' lives. For some, the lives they have led as teachers and teacher educators started out as half-chosen directions, as lukewarm alternatives to briefly considered careers in science and engineering, as casually made choices resulting in a lifetime of work. For some, the careers they chose and the lives they lived were the only ones they could see for themselves, given their economic and social status. Nearly all spoke of a sense of caring, and that teaching offered an opportunity not only to earn a living but also to contribute to society, an attitude they have carried into their present lives. Whatever the reasons, they found purpose and accomplishment in teaching.

No one in the sample interviewed cited as the major reason for entering teaching either of the two most frequently mentioned in the literature on teaching and often referred to by employers of teachers as desirable in prospective candidates: love of children and a desire to teach the discipline (Lortie, 1975). What does one make of this, for it is evident in their remarks that they are fond of teaching, that they like their current students. Perhaps they are so far from the early years of their teaching that they focus on things other than those near banalities. Or perhaps their current lives have led them to be more academically focused, less affectively oriented in their views of their careers, so that they choose to speak no longer of things like love of children. As I pointed out in Chapter 1, one of the problems with retrospective glances at the past is that time and experience cast their shadows over the events, and what is recalled may sometimes be as much a reflection of what one is now rather than what one was. All of the subjects in this study are mature, removed in time, and in most cases, place, from their first positions in education. One may remember what one did but not remember precisely why. I wonder what they would have answered had I asked what they see as the three most desirable qualities that first-year teachers should possess, if the platitudes about love of children and discipline mastery would have emerged. As for a desire to teach the discipline, most of the faculty interviewed who were once secondary school social studies, science, or mathematics teachers are now connected to the discipline, if at all, only through the teaching of methodology courses. Other than that, they are scholars of curriculum, classroom behaviors, and of other researchable areas.

Their remarks show that in some respects these faculty were like most of the teachers of their times in their selection of teaching in the lower schools as the point of entry into their careers. They perceived few alternatives; their choices may have been the results in part of their social and economic class. Yet they took considerable pleasure in their early professional years and look back on them with fondness.

Although they were like most teachers in many respects, they also proved to be different in their subsequent decisions to seek doctoral degrees and acquire positions in higher education. As we will see in Chapter 3, elements of chance entered these decisions as well, particularly for the senior faculty members in the study who came to enter higher education at a time of much opportunity. Yet in a sense, they are all "dropouts" from the teaching ranks of the lower schools. But they are a special kind of dropout in that they continued careers in education. In the next and ensuing chapters, I will describe their entries into the next career levels, their adaptations to a new environment, and their perceived contributions to the profession. We will see that for many the shift to higher education roles has provided a stronger sense of identity and degree of potency in their work. We will also see that they carried some potentially negative habits from their experiences in the lower schools into their lives as faculty in higher education institutions.

Although these 34 faculty may not be representative of all teacher educators in their choices to become teachers, the insights gleaned in interviews, the success of their own lives, and the pleasure they have taken in their early careers are valuable. There is currently much emphasis, perhaps rightly so, on the need for carefully structured programs for thoughtfully selected people to become the excellent teachers of tomorrow. If history repeats itself, some will teach a few years, go on for doctoral work, and become teacher educators in higher education. Their stories may someday be as compelling as those of the individuals in this study.

3 The Move to Higher Education

After I was first appointed to a higher education position, I didn't even know which cafeteria to eat in. But I liked the work right away. I had a chance to deal with ideas.

— *Male full professor*

As noted earlier, a criterion for inclusion of individuals in this study was several years of teaching experience in the public schools. This criterion is important for several reasons: most teacher educators have been teachers in the public schools (Ducharme & Kluender, 1990; RATE III, 1989; Lanier & Little, 1986; Ducharme & Agne, 1982), and I wanted that common background reflected in the study. How they viewed these early, formative years in their professional lives is important, for these views might have affected their decisions to enter higher education, their choice of academic study, and their behaviors in higher education. A male professor put it succinctly: "I loved teaching in the schools, but I went into university work because I thought I could better spend my time in preparing teachers than in teaching kids; you know, the influence would be broader." His remarks illustrate the long-term effect of the schooling experience on his views and his choice of work. Most of those interviewed desired to move from what had been a happy life to an unknown life that might be productive and professionally rewarding. They believed that they could make a difference in the education of teachers, a sentiment that echoes the belief many teachers hold about why they entered teaching; namely, to prepare students well (Lortie, 1975; Spencer, 1986; and Sikes, Measor, & Woods, 1985).

The views of these faculty about their earlier teaching are pervasively and consistently positive. Even those who described difficulties in their first couple of years spoke well of the time spent, for example, the male professor who observed: "The first couple of years were filled with problems, but I caught on to things and had a great time."

REASONS FOR LEAVING THE LOWER SCHOOLS

Despite their strong words, feelings, and commitments about their past happy days in the lower schools, they left. Why? Even though some had encountered difficulties in their early teaching, they unanimously reported that they had been successful teachers. Most left without a clear notion of what they might study in their doctoral work or what they would do after doctoral studies. Thus they left the security of a position in work they liked for an unknown future, one that did not guarantee a comparable level of happiness and accomplishment.

No Opportunities for Professional Development

Clearly, their fondness for teaching in the public schools had its limitations. When some of these individuals considered the long-term implications of staying in the classroom, they recoiled. The routinized life and work, the lack of reward differentiation for high performance, and the absence of personal freedom became important. For an untenured female science educator, staying in the schools was an unacceptable future:

> I finished my master's and did eight years of public school teaching and thoroughly enjoyed it, but I guess the main reason I got out was the reward for doing a good job was not there. Financially and in every other way it didn't matter if I was a really good teacher or not. I was going to get the same salary, the same fringe benefits, the same everything, except many a little bit of internal satisfaction as the fellow who was not doing a very good job.

Ironically, her sentiments about equal reward for unequal performances were later echoed by a male professor of reading, except that he was talking about how unequal departments are at his university.

> The legislature gives a set amount of percentage, and it gets awarded within departments. This department is very productive. When the raises come out we aren't rewarded the way we should be. In another department, not nearly as productive, a mediocre performance would get a better increase than someone here who is much more

productive because the level of performance in this department is so high. So I say to the administration: you want departments to distinguish between levels of faculty performance. Why don't you do the same with departments? Don't give the same to all departments. Do it on the basis of departmental performance. But they won't do it. I'm not hurting for money, but it's the principle of the thing. The increase is what people judge you on.

The female science educator may not find all the salary issues satisfactory at the university. However, she had other concerns in the schools: the inability to communicate with colleagues, the sense of isolation, and the growing feeling of being "bogged down" by the process of schooling became increasingly important:

> Plus the rigidity of the schedule. You can't go out to lunch, you can't go to the bathroom, you can't do anything. You just don't have a chance to communicate with any other professionals, even teachers in your school. If you do happen to have a planning period together or lunch period together, then you're usually so bogged down you don't want to talk professional things. It's a real problem—you're isolated. Your professional contacts are extremely limited. But I enjoyed the public school teaching, I really did.

The irony inherent in her remarks—the pervasive loneliness and the lack of contact with other adults in a profession ostensibly intended to improve communications—had echoes. For a former social studies professor, now a dean, the lack of professional colleagueship—a concern closely allied to not being able to communicate with others—was also an important reason:

> I was already conscious that the next five years were going to be like the last five years, and I said that I feel there's more about education that I would like to know. And I probably, I don't know if I articulated it, but I probably began to say something like the teachers I work with don't talk much about education or improvement or that sort of thing.

His statement of the "next five years" being like the "last five years," of course, echoes the feeling of sameness, the repetition that affects the long distance teacher. A female assistant professor observed a similar fear of being trapped into a life of sameness:

In public school teaching, when I looked across the pod, the lady there had been teaching for 17 years, and she was pulling out the same files she'd been using for years. I couldn't see myself doing that; I couldn't envision myself in the same room, doing exactly the same thing or similar things with children the rest of my life.

A male full professor commented that during his second year of teaching in the public schools a 30-year veteran English teacher offered to share the teaching outlines he had been using for all those years. The faculty member noted that he had suddenly become frightened that he would turn out the same way and decided that he was not going to make a career of teaching high school English: "The mere thought of all those outlines on the shelf gave me the chills."

These three faculty reflected in their unique ways the sentiments Sizer (1984) expresses about lack of variety in teachers' professional careers:

When people succeed, they want both increased challenges and the opportunity to assist others to master their craft. There is little scope for these natural desires in school work. How many people, save those of great self-possession, feel good about doing almost the same task at the day of retirement as they did on the first day of work? One can take enormous pleasure both at the mastery one may have developed and particularly at the students' lives one has touched, but the sameness of professional life for teachers gives little incentive for recognized excellence and influence, those powerful fuels for self-esteem. (pp. 186–87)

Isolation

Isolation has for a long time been an issue in the schools; teachers have frequently not had the opportunity to interact with one another nor with others in the community. A female tenured associate professor of special education addressed the question of isolation. Her recollections of her elementary school teaching days were a mixture of pleasure and isolation, a feeling of a lack of freedom. "I guess it was more the isolation than anything else, no going to lunch with a friend. You were just there with those children, which was fun."

Another female associate professor said that she feared she was losing her identity as she noticed that she was beginning to talk like a third grader, inasmuch as she was spending all her time with third graders. "I was with them all the time, and I noticed that I was beginning to sound like one of them. Much as I loved them, I knew that was not good."

A male senior foundations faculty member found that the climate of the schools eventually became stultifying:

> I guess the intellectual hunger was not being satisfied and a few teachers would talk and meet. It [the high school] was dominated by the old guard. There was a chair that belonged to an old teacher. I can remember that he died while I was there, and it took about a month before anyone sat in his chair.

He went on to indicate how talk of sports generally dominated the faculty-room conversation.

Lack of Planning Time

For others it was the "busyness" of the schools, the unrelenting tyrannies of time and bells that produced dissatisfaction. A female full professor observed that her public-school days were far too busy to allow her to plan, to make provisions to do the kind of teaching she wanted to do. The very activity that the schools demanded of this conscientious person meant that she could not prepare to do the kind of teaching that she valued. In addition, she needed more time in her professional development; she had a desire to work more with adults.

> As a public school teacher I didn't have any time at all for planning. I was there in class with kids the whole day. I had no opportunity to grow. I was on a committee to try to get planning time from the board, but they didn't do it. That's another reason I became active in the community; I wanted to interact with adults.

Her last remark echoes that of the former third-grade teacher who feared she was becoming childlike as a consequence of spending all of her time with children. A male associate professor also noted how he had never had enough time when he was teaching in the public schools:

> I've always lacked time to do what I want. I worked in a factory as a kid so I know what it is to punch a time clock, so I know what it's like to work a regular day. As a teacher, I can never remember ever having enough time, whether in elementary or secondary education.

I will discuss in Chapter 6 how limited amounts of time became a problem for some of these teachers once they were in higher education.

Structured Nature of the Schools

The formidable structure of the schools and its occasional debilitating effect on faculty were also causes of unsettledness. A female assistant professor in special education with past experience as a special educator in the public schools lamented the frustration in working through the structure in the schools:

> I think it was frustrating for me as a practitioner that there was a bureaucracy to deal with. And in special education there is a real large group to deal with, a real hierarchy to get kids placed. And I didn't like that; I became real frustrated with it. Moving into higher education was a real improvement for me professionally.

She was a victim of the bureaucracy that Sizer (1984) describes,

> Bureaucracies lumber. Once regulations, collective bargaining agreements, and licensure get installed, change comes hard . . . hierarchical bureaucracy stifles initiative at its base. . . . One sees it in the demoralization of many teachers and in the explanations able college students give for not taking up high school teaching as a career. (p. 209)

A female associate professor had similar feelings about structure, which gave her similar misgivings. "As a classroom teacher, everything was too structured, everything was planned for us: when we'd go to PE, when we'd go to art. Although I did use my creativity. It was just a matter of the structure." One can substitute her word *creativity* for Sizer's *initiative*. In either case, the result is stifling.

A female science educator observed that freedom was the exciting thing about being in higher education.

> I have freedom in a lot of different ways, daily schedule freedom as well as the freedom to go to professional meetings and become active in professional organizations. Most public schools, including the ones I worked for, maybe if you begged, you could use personal days, maybe they would even let you have professional days, one or two a year. If you were really lucky they paid for a substitute for you, but otherwise you were on your own.

These faculty as teachers did not fit the norm that Broudy (1972) describes and the usual reaction to the top-down structure of the schools, "The single outstanding fact about teachers—especially in American public schools has been their docility. Until very recently it was tacitly understood that classroom teachers were to carry out policies and programs designed by administrators, and supervisors" (p. 41).

The faculty in the study, although giving no evidence of rebellion in their stories to me, chose to leave the system rather than continue to have others governing their lives. In passing, one notes with grim irony how little things have changed in most American schools since 1972 when Broudy published his text, despite his opening, "until very recently" phrasing. For many communities, "recently" is still to come.

INFLUENCES OF LOWER-SCHOOL TEACHING ON UNIVERSITY WORK

Despite their misgivings about the schools and their decisions to leave, these faculty repeated and repeated how important, how invaluable their lower-school experience was. Their time in the schools ranged between only three and seven years, but that time continued to exert a powerful influence on the faculty during their careers. They tended to speak of the experience in near hyperbolic terms. For a female assistant professor in foundations, it was critical. "It's probably the most important thing I ever did as far as my impact on teacher education; it gave me understanding and also realism in that when I help students translate theory into practice, I have some reality to base my remarks on."

For a male science educator, just the experience of having done public school teaching has, according to him, stood him in good stead in both his teaching and his consulting:

> I think it's very difficult to relate to or get involved with prospec-
> tive teachers if you haven't had that experience. Just knowing
> what it is to survive in that environment is valuable. I can't think
> of a single way in which the experience has not been helpful. I use
> that experience a lot when I do consulting with public schools.

A male full professor also thought the experience had stayed with him his entire professional life:

> Well, it extremely influences you. Decisions about what I would say
> and do probably even to this day, the specific approach I take to su-
> pervision would be so different without that kind of experience, spe-
> cially the kind of experience I had in the Texas panhandle, stays with
> you.

A male professor commented, "Those years were 'chuckful' years. They helped me understand kids with a wide range of variability; it really did. I understand the kids here better as a result." For a male professor of reading, his teaching days, while pleasurable and rewarding, had also been marked by uncertainty about his success with young people; he chose his doctoral emphasis in part to become competent in what he thought he had not done well:

> I can still call up very specific instances during those years, things which I occasionally did well, but most of the time I was perplexed as to what was the right thing to do. I did the best that I could and the one thing that bothered me was the upper grade kids who came into the classroom not knowing how to read; I didn't know what to do. So when I went back to get my doctorate, I specialized in reading.

A male full professor in science education believed that the teaching he did in the public schools made him a better teacher at the university, a belief several others alluded to but not as explicitly as he did:

> Then I found teaching at the university level was not that different from teaching at the upper elementary grades. Oh, there are differences obviously, but still the whole need to empathize with students, to be structured, to have objectives . . . it's all the same. That was a bit of a surprise to me.

A NEW LIFE

These faculty had indeed served their time in the lower schools, and they could not help but be influenced by those years. The transition to higher education might well be marked by residue habits accumulated during the time as teachers. The schools have, as several of the interviewees observed, a powerful control over the daily lives of teachers and students. Several years ago, a colleague and I commented on that aspect of schooling and the contrasting condition in higher education.

> Even in those instances in which public school teachers find themselves with unassigned time such as lunch time or a "free" period, they are generally not to leave the building. . . . The work life is managed by forces external to teachers' lives.
>
> By contrast, professorial life in the universities is one managed more by

individual faculty members themselves than by institutionally or professionally set standards. (Ducharme & Agne, 1982, p. 33)

Freedom and Opportunities

A new life of self-direction, of autonomy, would have to replace the previous life of little self-management, of control by bells and schedules. Faculty did not always find the transition easy, but they generally welcomed it once they had accommodated to it. A female assistant professor indicated that higher education with all its freedom was appropriate now, but that she would have been unprepared for it earlier. "For this time in my life, the age I'm at now, this [higher education] is better. But I think at an earlier time that I would not have enjoyed it as much. I don't think that I would have sat down and done what I do now. I would not have been able to organize myself." Yet all did not find it difficult, even at first. Another female assistant professor stated: "I immediately liked the autonomy, the individualization. I certainly like being able to do different things."

The life in higher education is very different from life in the public schools. A male foundations professor observed:

> High school teaching is work; this is close to leisure; that's the difference. If we could make sure that we never forget that. The lifestyle, the amount of time we have, the sense of obligation it brings to do our best. These institutions are paying us, after all.

A male professor of reading echoed his thoughts:

> But the great freedom of teaching at the university level. We do it day by day without stopping to appreciate the great freedom that we have. We don't have to get there when the buses get there, we don't have to eat lunch when the students eat lunch, we go home when we want to. The great freedom to organize your own schedule! If you want to work 40 hours one week and 60 the next, nobody says anything. It's a great freedom.

Freedom is a recurring theme. A female foundations assistant professor found the freedom exhilarating:

> And on the days I'm not teaching, I don't have to come in if I don't want to. I can stay home and I can write and do my work. What I find, though, is that I work 12 to 14 hours on

those days and on weekends; they're getting their money's worth out of me.

A male professor stated clearly the difference in self-esteem that came about as a result of the change to higher education and the sense of personal liberation it engendered:

My whole concept of education just exploded. I grew up in a very rural county; my teaching experience was all there. I didn't know that anyone in the world would be interested in hiring me with that background. Then I found out they were interested, that I could go anywhere I wanted to. That was the first thing that hit me. Then once I got into college teaching, and I began to associate with people whose names I'd heard of and read about and realized that they didn't know the same things I didn't know. So I began to expand the area in which I thought, wide areas I wouldn't have dared to before because people wouldn't have been interested in what I had to say. The whole world just exploded.

For most of the faculty, higher education clearly meant a new and different way of living. Higher education had a mystique about it, something quite different from the public schools, something esoteric:

When I was a freshman or sophomore [in college], I was walking down the hall of the social science building, and those guys were in their offices putting posters over their windows and they were sitting there smoking their pipes and I said that these guys have the best life that is imaginable. And I remember how envious I was at the time but I don't think I seriously considered that I'd ever be able to do that.

Fifteen years later, after public-school teaching, marriage and three children, a master's degree, followed by three years of doctoral work, this individual, who is now a full professor, assumed an assistant professorship. Now, 20 years into his job at the university, he says he is happy, that it was all worth it.

These individuals were clear in their view that working in higher education is a privilege, a special way of life with implied responsibilities. They were not alone in their appreciation of the freedom of university life; many appeared to luxuriate in the liberty that faculty life gave them—the chance to do writing and research, the time to read, the frequency of exchange with colleagues, the opportunity to go to conferences and meet peers from other institutions; indeed, for most of the faculty interviewed, work in higher education was very much a new life.

Obligations and Responsibilities

A combination of altruism, a sense of knowing what was right, and professional commitment was part of the mix of reasons and feelings accompanying some decisions to leave and embark on a new life. As one male professor observed, "I thought I might be able to prepare teachers who would do a better job than some of my colleagues were doing." However self-serving and rationalizing that comment may appear, many share the sentiment, a feeling that may have lent a sense of obligation for some as they went into their new lives at new places with new associates. This attitude of obligation, of course, parallels some of the expressed reasons for initially entering teaching. The notion of setting the world aright is perhaps common to many young people as they start their careers. It is interesting that this feeling stayed with these faculty even as they began a second career in higher education.

This new life also carried with it new obligations and responsibilities. The attitudes that had characterized their earlier lives in the public schools remained; the focus for them had changed. They had, after all, found teaching to be a career in which they could help others, teach material, and contribute to the amelioration of human problems. These sentiments continued. A female assistant professor expressed it thus, "I feel such a sense of responsibility to these young teachers when they go out into the schools; I just hope that I've been able to help prepare them properly."

Along with the desire to contribute to the general good and the specific actions that this desire produced, faculty also wondered how good they were. Some questioned the efficacy of their efforts:

> I just never knew if what I was doing was the best thing for these young people; I never felt right in sending them out into the schools. I wasn't sure that they were prepared enough for what they were going to do, that I had done enough for them.

A female assistant professor worried that her former students would find her assistance not long lasting, adequate, or strong enough. She feared that the culture of the schools would overwhelm her work with her students:

> I think I'm more disillusioned now than I was when I was teaching in the schools. I said that I'm a really good teacher; I'm beginning to

question what kind of impact I'm having. I'm following my students more now, and I'm hearing them excuse things that are just poor practice. My impact doesn't last very long. They'll say "You taught us that paddling was an inappropriate managing technique but I found that it's the only thing that works." I get upset . . . I see them regress into the culture they're in and internalize some of their supervisor's bad habits . . . I'm getting into a state of disillusionment where I think maybe the problem is me. They're sitting in this class, they nod their heads, they discuss. But when I see them teach, or two years after they start teaching, it's like I never taught them anything. Maybe after they've taught a while, they might go back to some of those things, maybe.

Her plaintive observations evoke the sentiment in the remarks from the male professor quoted earlier in this chapter in which he observed, "I thought I could better spend my time in preparing teachers than in teaching kids." This professor thought so as well, but life in higher education is like life in the lower schools: not always predictable. Some things go well and some do not.

There was an occasional wondering about the lack of accountability in higher education, the other side of the freedom coin, a feeling that perhaps some individuals were not always acting responsibly.

The biggest surprise to me was the lack of accountability in higher ed. I could not believe it—I still am very—I'm uncomfortable with that—I certainly don't see myself as a hard head or extremely conservative in terms of being an administrator. . . . But I really feel like that the least we can do is ask people what have you accomplished? I think that professionally and just as a matter of ethics we owe the taxpayers, we owe the university, the fact that we are in higher education is special and I think that we owe our best to that heritage. I'm the only person in my family ever to finish a baccalaureate. I think it is real calling to fulfill the promise of what a university can and should be doing. To let people wander around making 35 or 40 or 50 thousand a year with no accountability, I don't think that's very wise.

The sense of obligation to higher education, to the state, and to the profession, however vaguely defined, was a recurring theme. Some had transferred the early idealism that had characterized their enthusiasm for teaching in the lower schools to a sense of responsibility about their work in higher education. This sense of obligation came out in a variety of ways and views: perseverance in their duties, loyalty to their employing institutions, and service for the profession. In general, it was older faculty, those in their late forties and fifties, who expressed these views.

CONCLUSION

The thoughts about public school teaching the faculty in my study expressed are similar to some of those expressed by the teachers in Lortie's (1975) study, in which they observed that in teaching, "I just think you sort of stagnate in a way," (p. 98), or "I think in other occupations you may meet more people with different interests" (p. 97). The desire to be involved with significant people, the wish to continue to grow and learn — these are constants through the decades. One of the differences between the subjects in Lortie's study and those in this study is that the latter actually made career shifts and moved from the public schools to advanced degree work and to positions in higher education, while the former continued in their public school teaching careers.

There is much call recently to recruit the best and the brightest into teaching. The arguments for recruitment of prospective teachers from this range of students run the gamut from the alleged benefits the young would get from being taught by such individuals, to how the nation would benefit in terms of improved education for all. The lives of the individuals in this study have some meaning for this argument, for they were among the "best and the brightest" of those entering teaching. It is interesting to note that no faculty members in their occasionally rambling responses to my remarks and questions indicated any sustained effort on their parts to change the schools in which they were placing their students, but rather addressed the matter of how they might prepare their students well to work and survive in the schools. There were, to be sure, faculty who castigated the schools for their performance, their treatment of children, and so forth, but gave little attention to themselves as possible reformers.

They left public-school teaching because of isolation, low autonomy, poor intellectual climate, fear of becoming boring to students, and lack of personal time. A cursory reading in the literature on present schooling in America reveals that the same conditions generally prevail. Even if the schools could recruit more of the best and the brightest, lacking fundamental changes in teaching conditions, the schools will be no more effective at retaining such teachers than they have been in the past decades.

And thus they left. But they did not forget their years in the lower schools.

4 Research and Publication

I've enjoyed publishing and then having people write and inquire about my work. That's been, for whatever reason, very exciting. I just love to see my name in print.

— *Female tenured associate professor*

The nature and quality of faculty research and scholarship in schools, departments, and colleges of education and particularly among teacher education faculty have been problematic for a long time.

> Teacher educators are in a difficult position with respect to scholarly productivity, the traditional trademark of the university professor. It has been noted that professors of education, as a general rule, rarely follow up on the work begun during their doctoral studies. Indeed, for some who have produced projects rather than the more traditional research based dissertation, there may be nothing, in fact, to follow up on. (Ducharme, 1986a, p. 57)

Although the need for a definition of academically respectable, viable research and scholarship exists in all the academic disciplines, it is particularly needed in teacher education, if only because of the frequent brickbats critics hurl at it. Despite what detractors may say, teacher-education faculty do conduct research, do publish in journals, do write scholarly books, and do make presentations at national conferences as a result of peer review and juried selection. But even those within the profession raise questions about the quality of the scholarship of teacher-education faculty. Schwebel (1989), after acknowledging that education faculty may publish as much as faculty in other disciplines, notes that "a qualitative measure would be preferable, but the quantitative standard should not be disparaged. . . . Quantity is a necessary, although not sufficient criterion" (p. 55), thereby questioning the value of some education faculty research. Howey and Zimpher (1990) also raise the quantity-quality issue:

Better understanding of present teacher education contexts in terms of both constraining and enabling factors is needed to point the way for how to study faculty scholarship in the future. More accurate assessments of the *quality*, as well as quantity, of present research undertaken in different contexts and with different purposes in mind is but needed baseline data. (p. 358)

Although such has not always been the case, current teacher education faculty must meet the research and scholarship requirements to survive in higher education. Wisniewski (1989) argues the point forcefully:

Despite the interminable debate about the matter, a commitment to scholarship, the essence of university life, must characterize those who prepare teachers. Those among our ranks who do not share this commitment contribute to our second-rate status in the academy. (p. 135)

Lawson (1990) notes that there has been an ever-increasing emphasis on research and scholarship, a trend that he believes has taken away from the service commitment of SCDE faculty. He describes three types of education faculty: practitioners-turned-professors, practitioner-scholars, and professional scholars (p. 61). The degree to which this is an applicable depiction of teacher-education faculty may be debatable, but the distinctions are useful. The faculty in this study fall more or less within the three categories.

All the faculty interviewed for this study made the transitions from teaching and administering in the public schools to studying for a doctoral degree, to seeking and finding positions in higher education, and to making the adjustments necessary to succeed in the new environments.

Several individuals in the study had entered their doctoral work with intentions of returning to the lower schools once they had finished their doctorate: "I wanted to learn more about teaching and then return to the classroom." None of them did. No one knows what tricks of the mind it took to decide to abandon a work environment in which they had been successful for a number of years, in which they had colleagues and friends, in which they knew the necessary survival skills. No interviewee was articulate on this point. The most that any could say was a vague statement about how it seemed the right thing to do at the time. Several appeared to have guilt qualms about their decisions. "I sometimes wonder if I shouldn't have stayed in high school teaching."

They may have been unprepared to meet the demand for research and scholarship when they began their careers in higher education, in part as a result of their previous experiences in the lower schools, where there are no such expectations. Clifford and Guthrie (1988) describe the dilemma that many education faculty live out:

For all their numbers, education faculty are an intellectually fragmented group, more divided into "sects" than their nineteenth century medical counterparts. . . . Some [faculty] are former elementary or secondary school teachers or administrators, who have carried a particular orientation into the college and university world. (p. 40) . . . Drawn to higher education less to promote scholarship and doctoral education than to improve the quality of schooling by teaching future teachers, they are likely to spend longer hours on the campus in teaching and advising than on research projects. (p. 88)

Clifford and Guthrie's comments echo what Agne and I observed about education faculty who had spent a long time in the schools,

It is questionable whether or not SCDE faculty have, generally speaking, ever learned effective management of their time in higher education. . . . Some faculty members will regularly be in their offices from 8:30 to 4:30 except on those days when they teach a late class; then they come in a little later but still manage to work a full day, at least by comparison with their earlier work habits. (Ducharme & Agne, 1982, p. 33)

Each career transition has personal issues for the individuals making it. For these former teachers, the decision to study for a doctoral degree had issues of personal and professional credibility. The decision to return to higher education likely was a matter of conscience for some in that it was a decision to participate in a process that they may have earlier disparaged, the relevancy of study in graduate institutions of education to their own professional lives. In their decision-making period, these faculty may have had views similar to those held by the teachers Cohen (1991) studied, one of whom observed:

"The basic problem with these ed courses," Bill says of his experience at T. C., "is overkill. There *are* some things that are worth reading, that can help a young person get ready for the classroom. But mixed in with the valuable stuff is so much bullshit, so much filler—things that are self-evident or not useful at all. The whole master's program could have been condensed into a couple of courses." (p. 65)

These faculty, for some of the reasons cited in previous chapters, were returning to a source that they had once not favorably regarded. In fact, one of the faculty commented that when he finished his master's degree in the late 1950s he had said, "I will never be on the student side of the desk again, never take another course in education." Another noted that she had had little use for the "ramblings of education writers from universities." Now they, like the rest, were on the other side of that metaphorical desk, teaching people about teaching and being forced or going eagerly or willingly to the tasks of writing and publishing. Now they would have to produce some scholarly work.

SCHOLARLY RESEARCH AND PUBLICATION: PROBLEMS AND ISSUES

Once they made the decisions to pursue their futures in higher education, these former schoolteachers then had to find faculty positions; when they had accomplished that, they then had to do the necessary adapting to fit into this new environment. In the previous chapter, I observed how the faculty saw the changes in how they spent their time in higher education, the flexibility of a self-determined schedule, the freedom of higher education as major differences between life in the lower schools and in higher education institutions. Yet with these freedoms came a new responsibility: scholarly research and publication. How some faculty interpreted or chose to interpret this responsibility differed somewhat in the various types of institutions, the period of time during which they entered higher education, their own experience in obtaining their doctorate, and the degree to which they had been mentored into the appropriate role for a higher education faculty member. All save one agreed that they were expected to do research and publication, albeit to different degrees. Some were puzzled by this expectation, uncertain about how to fulfill it, what it meant, and its validity. These faculty in their sometimes unfocused responses about research and publishing fulfilled the varied descriptions of education faculty scholarship implicit in many studies, namely that much is unfocused, uneven, and lacking in traditional rigor (Howey & Zimpher, 1990; Judge, 1982; Ducharme & Agne, 1982).

Ambiguities

The published work of professors of teacher education is extraordinarily uneven. Some of the work, for example, that of Doyle (1986), Gideonse (1989), Zeichner (1986), would fulfill any definition of academic research and scholarly writing. Other writing, including speculative essays on the future of teacher education, descriptions of what individuals do in particular programs, futuristic looks at schooling, and so forth, is considerably more controversial and defies conventional yardsticks. Yet all of this and more is present in what professors report in Agne's and my study (Ducharme & Agne, 1982) and in the annual RATE surveys. All manner of items appear under the rubric of "refereed publications," ranging from a description in a state journal of how an elementary teacher preparation program might be changed to an analysis of a highly sophisticated study of the effects of field experiences on first year education students appearing in a national journal with a scholarly panel of reviewers. Many SCDE promotion and tenure committees have pondered the relative merit of textbooks and the like versus articles in refereed journals.

A male math educator in his late fifties expressed the ambiguities that inhere in SCDEs relative to scholarship and publication:

> Oh, I did a little bit of writing. Put together some presentations, always did something at ATE and that sort. It seemed to do the trick. But as far as substantive work, I didn't do any. And I'm just now getting going. I wiped out pretty well earlier. In the last year—the most interesting and really thoughtful experience that I've had in scholarship—I arranged myself, by golly, a swap off with a guy over in England. I got a couple of good articles out of that. And now I'm beginning some work in teacher thinking and that is what I've been spending a good bit of my time with. Most of the stuff I did earlier, and I've got a couple of pages of it on my vitae, but it's pretty thin, pretty thin, pretty descriptive. I'm not satisfied with the depth of what I've been able to do. I may go down in flames. But when I get some answers I think they are going to be substantive. I really do.

A male science educator articulated another of the ambiguities of scholarship and research in schools, colleges, and departments of education when he commented that he was not doing research, but merely writing:

> I think it would be more accurate to say that I do *writing*, not research. The drive to do "research" came initially from a grant, and I was in charge of doing some things. I had gotten involved with new social studies curriculum materials, the Hilda Taba stuff; I got to be known as a trained expert in her material. But most of my publications are just writing, not scholarship.

These experiences nonetheless led him to the co-writing of textbooks and how-to projects. Similarly, a male professor of reading lamented that he had not done the "serious" scholarship that he had wanted to do when he first entered the professoriate; he felt he had merely done textbooks and such. Both of these faculty commented that their decisions, while perhaps not the most academic decisions they might have made, worked to their fiscal advantage.

Sources of Impetus

Nearly half of the faculty in this study saw themselves as the main impetus for their drive to conduct research, write, and publish. Although they were unable to tell specifically what in them that produced this urge, they nevertheless cited it as primary.

A male professor of science education was clear that it was his own initiative that got him started on doing scholarly work:

> Why did I publish? My own personal pressure. It was a change coming here 20 years ago. I realized that promotion is tied in with research and publication and those kinds of things. I somewhat fought it for a while. I wanted to do teaching and service. In fact, I didn't apply for graduate school faculty status for years because of that. I sometimes regret the pressure on publications and research and the less attention given to teaching. We are supposedly a research institution. I've fought it myself.

Another male teacher educator had similar expectations about himself:

> Well, I had always wanted to, when I became a college professor I was in my upper thirties and I promised myself that I wanted to do three things: one, I wanted to teach; two, I wanted to do something in my field. I was too late to become a renowned scholar, but I wanted to be respected in my field, and three, I wanted to be of service to the university and the community.

But he did begin writing and did some publishing because "I wanted to."

A male professor of reading cited his compulsion, a trait similar to the self-starting characteristic of the previously cited science education faculty member:

> Well, I'm a compulsive researcher, writer. When I came here in 1966, I said to the dean that I knew this was a publish or perish school, so I said to the dean, what does it take to survive here? He asked me what I'd been doing. I said about five or six publications a year, and he said that will do here. I said okay, and that that's what I did with no pressure whatsoever. I've got about 250 things in print; the vitae's about 25 pages long. I've been a full professor for about 20 years.

A tenured male associate professor in secondary education at a large state university also stated that his own drive was the compelling force:

My own initiative when I began. I'd get some ideas that I thought were important and deserved to be said. I'd write them up and send them off. It took discipline. I got a lot of good feedback on them; that was a good incentive to do more. I've done some joint publishing. I expect to get promoted pretty soon. I think the whole state has raised the ante for being promoted. I realized a few years ago that it wasn't automatic anymore. I got caught up in the expectations being raised. Oh, for a while it was getting a couple of articles a year published, being involved in national presentations. All these things I was doing. Then they raised it to having to do a book. Well, I'm waiting—finally—to find out if I'm being promoted to full professor. That's after 22 years!

A female full professor and department chair said that she was very self-motivated:

It's also your self-esteem. As a full professor—which I am—if you're not into research, you don't feel good about yourself. I've always been interested and active in scholarship, but my work has always been more applied. Now there's a push to be involved in basic research, whatever that is.

A male foundations professor indicated that, early in his career, he had a commitment to write and do scholarly work, but that it had not made much difference initially, as his casual observations about how others viewed his work indicate:

And the dean didn't seem to give a damn one way or the other. In fact, for the most part, his long-term concern was not to be aware very much of what people were doing. And I've published, but no brilliant record, but regularly, a couple of things a year, sometimes five or six. As best as I can tell, I guess it was appreciated; I got good marks and good evaluation.

This individual clearly experienced uncertainty about the value of his work. When I asked why he did it he commented:

I really don't know what motivates me. I think it's my expectation of the role of the professor. It's part of the university. They are paying you, you are teaching nine hours a week. What do you do if you don't do it? If there were no expectations, I don't know if I'd do it, because it's damned hard work.

He may have inadvertently explained why he did research and scholarship at a later point when he commented that his dissertation supervisor had written in a letter of recommendation that he (the faculty member) "was a damned hard worker who enjoys research and you can expect lots of publications out of him."

The Influence of Advisers and Colleagues

For other faculty, the urge to conduct scholarly work came from their doctoral advisers and was sustained by associates and colleagues. A female tenured associate professor in special education at a large private university observed that:

> The drive comes largely from my doctoral work, the environment there. Not only did I have an adviser, a mentor, but there was also a group of students who all worked very collaboratively with each other. We still do even though we are in different institutions. Sometimes we did research with faculty; other times we did it with ourselves.

Simeone (1987) notes, "Even lesser institutions, while realizing that many of their faculty will never be as prolific as world-renowned scholars, value and reward research productivity" (p. 52). As one interviewee expressed the matter, "It's everywhere." A male tenured associate professor in teacher education at a small liberal arts institution also spoke of the importance of his doctoral work toward his becoming a scholar and noted the need to work with colleagues:

> I think I brought the interest in doing research with me; it probably reflects my doctoral graduate work more than anything else. It just interests me; I like to do that kind of stuff. I'm probably more empirically oriented than anyone else in the department. Recently, for a couple of reasons, a colleague in the developmental area, sort of needs to do some stuff for her tenure and I asked her last year if she was interested in picking up on the study of kids in solving word problems, which I sort of started last year. I saw that there was just a lot of territory to explore and a great opportunity with the school do to it. This is the first time I've had the opportunity to collaborate with someone in the department. It makes a big difference having somebody else thinking about the very same stuff. You find that you come up with a lot more ideas too.

He also commented that the combination of the institution's small size with its proclaimed commitment to the liberal arts and the teaching of its faculty meant that he did not have many colleagues with whom he could work on research.

It was the graduate-committee chair who played a pivotal role for a male science educator:

> I feel a lot of pressure to do that [research]. But mostly pressure from myself. My chairman of my committee got me started on that in his graduate classes for both his master's and doctoral students. As one of assignments he would require that we submit a given number—one, two, or three—articles for possible publication. He would see that you at least get them submitted a few places and give us guidance in polishing and submitting them. Most of us had at least one article published in a refereed journal by the time we left. In fact, the very first article I had published in the *Science Teacher* resulted in a publisher writing and saying we really like this article, would you like to do a book for us. I said, "Gee, is this the way it works?" I did the book.

The Influence of Leadership

While the value of administrative leadership in SCDEs may be subject to question, there may, however, be some subtle ways in which these leaders do influence what happens in their institutions. Certainly some of the faculty in this study expressed the idea that a dean or a chair's influence played a significant part in their performance in research and publishing. For some, changes in leadership can make a difference in their perceptions about the value of scholarship. A male foundations professor expressed the idea that, even though he had been publishing regularly without much recognition, "Then the dean and chair came. It's made some difference, too. That kind of work is appreciated now."

A male tenured professor in science education at a major southern university also found support for his work with the coming of a new dean.

> When the new dean came, he talked about colleges of education and scholarship, and he said that he didn't care if you don't do anything but go out and ask your student teachers some questions. And you come back and meet with some colleagues up here in the faculty lounge and bring a bag lunch and discuss what happened. At least

you can do that. At least get up out of your coffin and breathe – do something. That can be the beginning of scholarship.

A senior male science education professor at a large private university shared similar sentiments:

> Well, when I was hired here the primary concern was on my teaching. But things changed along about 1979; we got a new dean. And as time has gone by the onus to publish has become stronger and stronger. So that it has become one of the prime elements of professional load. And, of course, they want everything else to be excellent: your teaching and your advising. But what determines raises around here is your scholarship. I'm making my adjustments, paying more attention to the publishing and research aspects. The rules of the game have changed to a certain extent; if you want to survive, you've got to change with them. And I can understand all that in terms of what publishing does. I let "busyness" get in the way of scholarship. Oh, I did a little bit of writing, but not enough.

A male retired chair and former professor of social studies education commented both on his own research and his sometimes frustrating efforts to promote quality educational research as opposed to disciplinary research, which had been the focus of the historians and geographers in his department, individuals who resisted pedagogical research either by themselves or by new faculty.

> Partly from myself, partly because of research done for my master's thesis and doctoral dissertation. And I don't mean to make much of my book; it was just a re-working of my doctoral dissertation, certainly no great shakes, but it *was* a book. First of all, I think my role was to convince people who came out of the schools to our department that they could do research, whether they were master's or doctoral students. Of course, the new faculty who came in had to be integrated into our way of thinking. Of course, we had such a varied group that it was pretty easy to do. I would say, "Well, you can buddy up with George or somebody." The culture was research oriented. The research was mostly discipline oriented. Very little research came out of my department that was professionally oriented. It was only when two women faculty came that we began to get good

research of a professional kind. But again, in talking about bringing these new people into the faculty fold, I don't think I succeeded very well. After fighting hard to get the people I wanted, who would do what I conceived as useful educational research, then I lost these people because the departmental culture was hostile to it.

In his last sentence the former department chairman illustrates how administrators cannot always sway the views of their departments. In this case, the more traditional scholars overruled the chairman's desire to change the pattern, to break the mindset of the department, to vary the scholarly direction. His belief that teachers coming from the lower schools to study in master's and doctoral programs could do quality research predates the current emphasis on teachers as researchers by 30 years, for the period to which he was referring was the late 1950s and the 1960s.

Unfocused Scholarship and Regrets

Many of the preceding statements illustrate what several faculty expressed, namely, a lack of focus and a wandering about on their own, seeking scholarly focus. Often, when I inquired about who was setting the direction for such work, they responded simply that they had to do scholarly work, publish, and so forth, so that they found some area of interest and did it. They all had the general feeling that *something* must be done, so they did something the value of which they questioned later in life when they had accumulated some experience and a little wisdom. Their views on their early research and publishing reflect the frequent lack of focus in SCDEs, where individuals may take off and conduct inquiry or research in areas of interest to themselves but sometimes unrelated to the institutional mission.

The growing emphasis on the perceived "publish or perish" mentality at many institutions may have produced some of the unfocused scholarship for which some teacher-education faculty have a reputation. Several of the faculty in the study described how early in their careers they had simply done things, written articles with little apparent conviction or interest, but rather with a need to publish, to be visible in the so-called scholarly community or to get through the tenure process, the publish or perish syndrome. In their recollections of their earlier work, they attach little importance to it, seeing it as a means to an end rather than an end in itself. They now wonder about the quality of that earlier work. A female tenured associate professor in special education expressed the belief that now that tenure was hers she could be freer to do "important" work:

> When I fill out promotion papers, well, I'd like to be a full professor someday. One of the reasons is that there are so few women who are full professors. I wonder whether it's going to be longitudinal study, whether it's going to be interviewing like you're doing and take a long time. Before tenure, I felt pushed, go do it. Write it up; get it out. And it takes so long to get things published. The turn-around time on manuscripts is incredible. I have one coming out in *AERAJ* on research done three years ago. It took that long . . . three years! I read that study now and I'm not sure I even agree with it. Now that I have my tenure I want to worry about whether something is important or not instead of just doing something for the file. But not I find myself, instead of doing quick individual studies that I can get published in a hurry, I'm beginning to think of more in-depth things that will have more of an impact on education. I'm doing this more from an internal motivation of wanting to contribute to the field rather than have to worry about whether it looked good in my file or not.

She noted that earlier in her pretenure years that she had done studies and reported on them, but that she now no longer believed in that work.

> I don't believe in my own results anymore, of what I was really saying. It was too quick and fast. I'd spend eight hours training kids and then I'd say it had an effect. And it did; the statistics showed it. But then I'd go back in and do some interviews, find out what really happened. I think I became disgusted with the superficiality of my research, just sliding across the surface, and coming out with "significant" results. I'd like some better quality in my research.

The desire for "quality in my research" is an admirable virtue, yet one wonders how many instances of questioning or repudiating of earlier work there are among veteran faculty; further, one cannot help but relate that to some of the broader academy's views of some educational research and writing. Done in haste and without real conviction, how valuable can it be?

THE CLARITY OF NEW EXPECTATIONS

Pressure on New Faculty

For new faculty in the 1990s and beyond, the directions for professional scholarship may be clearer. Regardless of the appropriateness of inappropriateness of the emphasis on faculty careers and on SCDEs in general, deans, chairs, and provosts are making it evident to new faculty that they must be active scholars; certainly the junior faculty in this study report such to be the case. A female assistant professor in educational foundations indicated how clearly the expectations had been delineated for her when she arrived at the university:

> The provost made it very clear when we came in. . . . "Now we spent lots of money to bring you here. Like Harvard, we want you to get tenure here, the way you get tenure is to publish." My work is very good. It takes a long time to do it. It's ethnographic research. But the research itself is real sensitive because in this classroom I ask for their best first-grade teacher and then an ethnography—I'm up front about wanting to see the mechanism—how it's played out in the classroom. Well, it's devastating for the kids. The language the teacher used, the way she structured the whole classroom. "Don't do this. You can't do that. Orange group—I don't think you can do it either. But red and yellow can do this easily." I have ethnographic data I think is kind of sensitive. But I know what I have to do.

A male tenured associate professor of secondary education observed how things had changed and expressed the sentiment that, for new faculty, things are clearer now:

> Everything's laid out for new people now: you will have national presentations; you will have national publications; you will write grants. Every institution in the state has the same expectations. I'm happy to see that; I think there is a lot to be done.

A female assistant professor in special education indicated that she felt continual pressure to do writing, and that she feared that she would not have the time:

> Ha! It's always there. You walk down the hall and someone says, "How's the writing going?" What writing? I'm trying not to

be rude, but it's like I'm still preparing for new classes and supervising student teachers, and getting acclimated and writing—well, you need time. But it's very clear that I need to do it; the dean has made it very clear.

She also expressed concerns about whether or not she would make it through the system:

They're very clear. I have no doubts about what the criteria are. My doubts are whether or not I can meet them, what I have to give up in order to meet them. I'm beginning to question the system, not understanding what it means to be a university professor. Finding out what it means and then this is what I need to do. Maybe I'm a little late in this, maybe other people have a better sense of it. How am I going to do a sufficient amount of balance to satisfy these people here to be able to stay in a tenure-track position—if that's what I decide to do—and be able to do what I want to do personally. I don't want an exception; I want to do it right.

Another female assistant professor in early childhood at a four-year college expressed the clear knowledge of the necessity to do research and publishing but was uncertain about what the expectations were:

The pressure doesn't come from individual colleagues, but from some sort of common understanding; that is of the college. It's part of the profession. It's one of the things you do if you want to stay in or advance in the profession. I always find that the expectation is a little fuzzy at any place. It is perfectly clear, it is clear that you're expected to engage in scholarly work, which in some cases is research and in some cases a variation of that. But exactly the nature of that in order for it to be acceptable and a quantity of that in order for it to be acceptable is pretty fuzzy. Even here where somehow in my head I thought it might be easier to figure it out. I have no idea of what's appropriate.

The two previous quotations are in sharp contrast to the observation of a female full professor and department chair that the faculty joining higher education now are much better prepared for the rigors of scholarship. "Oh, they're better. They have richer backgrounds; they're better prepared as researchers. They're more specialists, more in-depth in certain areas. I think they do research and writing before they finish their dissertations."

Her comments on the new faculty suggests that some faculty are prepared to assume the role.

In 1986 I commented on the quality of recently prepared faculty:

> The growing number of new, research-trained Ph.D.s coming to SCDEs suggests that the next cohort of professors of education will come to higher education already enculturated into a research mentality. This condition suggests the existence of a core of individuals ready for this now more clearly needed and defined role. (Ducharme, 1986b, pp. 53–54)

Reactions of Older Faculty

What is requisite may often be clear, but for some older faculty there may be the feeling that things have changed too much, that they cannot do or choose not to do what is now expected. A senior male associate professor at a state university expressed the tensions several articulated:

> I suspect the pull of this institution is now in the direction of what the professors ought to be doing, that is, the publishing part. We're being pulled in a way that we have never been pulled before. Most of the people came here when that was not a requirement. And so we have seen efforts, extreme efforts to get us to do things we didn't believe in that strongly. This place had been largely teaching and student centered. But, I guess I'll do it. I've done some research, but not much. The pressure is on us, but research is not something we do terribly well. But research is such a broad term. I'm caught in the situation. I can see it from the dean's perspective. I went up for full professor last year and he turned me down. I just didn't have enough publications. I don't think it's entirely bad. I should have done more research and publishing; I know that.

This faculty member was echoing the views of Goodlad (1990) who, writing of the shift to greater emphasis on scholarship, noted that

> For many faculty members in all fields, weathering the shift in the balance of missions has been painful. . . . The older men and women left behind in teacher education also witnessed a decline in the status of the work they believed they could do well—and a frequent eschewing of this work by young colleagues advancing up the promotional ladder.
>
> Although this shift in mission has been most profound and pervasive in the regional universities, every college and university we visited was having to come to terms with it. The dislocations being caused by increased emphasis

on scholarly activity were now part of the recent history of the flagship public and private universities. There was little ambiguity with respect to expectations; new faculty members were almost always well informed before coming regarding work requirements. . . . Nevertheless, faculty members with no publications over the last two or three years were looking ahead with some apprehension to their next promotion review. (p. 193)

A male professor in teacher education caught up in the period of time to which Goodlad refers observed that:

> Well, in my first two years of teaching college, they were patient with me and didn't emphasize scholarship; they knew I was trying to get my teaching together. But they let me know that it was something that I would have to do. But when I came to this university, it was not emphasized, as a matter of fact, it was incidental. If you did it, it was okay, but the emphasis was on service, on work in the schools. I did a little bit of it, I published, I did a little research. But there was not pressure to do it. In fact, I was seen as a little odd for doing it. I wish I had done more the way things played out. But the new faculty have to do it all; there is pressure on them. If people have tenure and all they want to do is teach and do service, they can stay here. But if they want to get into the reward structure, merit pay and all that stuff, then they have to produce.

Another senior male faculty member and administrator found the situation quite different at a different type of institution and has successfully avoided serious research and scholarship:

> Well, we don't have the pressure for the kind of scholarship that is required in larger institutions. I'd be playing my life differently if we did. I could write and I will, but because of the tediousness of writing an article and getting it through, I just won't do it. But the kinds of writing skills I have, I know I could do it. I read for the *Journal of Teacher Education* and if I was under pressure and had to write three articles I believe that I could do it.

He also indicated his awareness of how things were changing, even in his regional university, when he subsequently observed, "I tell the new people here that they have to publish."

A male science educator clearly had "gotten through" the promotion process before things had changed. He is almost cavalier about matters of rank:

I sometimes regret the pressure on publications and research and less attention given to teaching. I attribute my emphasis to my early years in teaching. We are supposedly a research institution. I've fought it myself. When I go into the classroom, I want to do the best possible job that I can. Sometimes I feel as though I'm not doing the best job I can because of other pressures. I got promoted to full professor in the late 70s or the early 80s, I guess. The title doesn't mean much. But I felt I had to get promoted.

Another senior male professor, a faculty member in reading at a major institution with many publishing entries on his vitae, expressed rue over what he hadn't done as a researcher:

I'm still not a researcher. I really ought to be doing more research than I am, ought to have some research program that is ongoing. When I finished my doctoral degree I wanted to find out how children learn words, what goes in those little heads. But I didn't do that.

These faculty represent the range of views on and experiences in research and scholarship that one encounters in almost any SCDE. They reflect the variety that is both a richness and a plague, a richness in that the panoply of human variety is represented, and a plague in that the very panoply defies consistency of act and viewpoint.

It is axiomatic that not all faculty will be skilled writers and researchers. It is further axiomatic that not all faculty, including some who are skilled, will want to write and conduct meaningful research. Yet Wisniewski's (1989) injunction that "a commitment to scholarship, the essence of university life, must characterize those who prepare teachers" (p. 135) remains crucial.

The Need for Support

A few faculty express the need for support from other individuals in their research and writing. This was particularly the case if faculty had experienced support while pursuing their doctoral degrees; they wanted it to continue. For example, one female associate professor said, "Not only did I have an adviser, a mentor, but there was a group of students who all worked collaboratively with each other." The male associate professor cited above talked about the value of collaboration: "This is the first time I've had the opportunity to collaborate with someone in the department. It makes a big difference having somebody else thinking about the very same stuff. You find that you come up with a lot more ideas too." Collaboration implies colleagueship, a condition that may not often prevail. Troyer (1986) contends that, "Establishing professional collegiality appears to be a problem for teacher educators, especially for new professors" (p. 8). Brittingham (1986) argues that one of the major priorities for faculty development is to "develop the collaboration skills of faculty members" (p. 4). In Chapters 5 and 6, I will discuss the experiences and views of these faculty on mentoring and collaboration.

CONCLUSION

One cannot possibly generalize to the entire population of teacher education faculty from these 34 individuals. But some recurring themes from their views of and experiences with research and publication are worth noting.

It is surely no surprise that nearly all are aware of the pressure to be involved in scholarly work. What is surprising perhaps is the degree to which faculty in the present day feel this pressure irrespective of the size and type of institution in which they teach. As one assistant professor in a four-year college expressed it, "We're all expected to do *something*." Ambiguity about expectation appears to be present in smaller institutions as expressed in the comment of the female assistant professor in early childhood education who noted that "I have no idea of what is appropriate." A male associate professor expressed a sense of his uniqueness among older faculty at a liberal arts institution when he observed, "I'm probably more empirically oriented than anyone else in the department."

Some faculty question the quality of work they did earlier in their careers; a desire to do more important, more significant research accompanies this dissatisfaction. Some mature faculty express regret that they have not done more scholarly work in their careers. Quality of the research of teacher education and education faculty generally has long been an issue, as I indicated earlier in this chapter.

Finally, there is the desire to excel, to do work of enduring quality. This aspiration for excellence is visible in the comments of several faculty, but most particularly in the remark of the female faculty member who wants no breaks, no special treatment in her career, but only wants quality: "I don't want an exception; I want to do it right."

5 Mentoring and Collaborating

*Nothing satisfied him until it was right. He just didn't give someone a
low grade; he gave it back and made them do it again until they got it
right. And that taught me something that has, in a way, been a burden to me. I never felt that I could give a student a B-minus on a paper
and write a brief comment on it and give it back to him. It was just not
part of the culture I was developed in.*
—Male retired professor of social studies education

The concept of mentoring comes to us from the Greeks. The goddess
Athena took the form of the Ithacan noble Mentor in order to guide
Telemachus, the son of Ulysses, in his quest for manhood. It is interesting
that, even though Athena takes the form of a man to help Telemachus, it
is she, a female goddess, who is the real source of wisdom and help.
Thus the first mentor-mentee relationship recorded in literature was a
female-male one. Today one reads mostly of genderlike relationships being
advocated.

Generally speaking, the image of mentor is that of an experienced and
trusted counselor helping another person. I have been interested in the
possibilities of mentoring for teacher education faculty for some time. In
1987 I wrote a series of recommendations that universities might act on to
strengthen teacher education faculty. Among those recommendations was
this injunction:

Develop a mentor system whereby mature faculty work with new faculty. The late
1980s and the 1990s promise to be a time of modest growth in the numbers
of education faculty at many institutions. There will thus be a need to encul-
turate new faculty members. This need can best be met by mature faculty
working with young faculty in deliberate ways. (p. 86)

Thus I looked forward to learning of the mentoring experience of the faculty I interviewed.

It is useful in a discussion such as this to have a working definition of the term under scrutiny. Simeone (1987) presents an effective description of what a sponsor or mentor does or can do; she uses the terms *sponsor* and *mentor* interchangeably.

> The sponsor/protegé (or mentor/protegé) relationship has long been considered an important one in the academic world. The sponsor may serve many functions for the protegé. First, the sponsor introduces and initiates the protegé in the customs, demands, and expectations of academic life. Second, the sponsor shares his or her wisdom and knowledge with the protegé, and provides encouragement and comments on his or her work. Third, the sponsor can provide career assistance for the protegé by making recommendations to his or her colleagues at his or her institutions, or simply by sharing a bit of the deflected glow from his or her own shining reputation. Perhaps most important, the sponsor helps to form within the protegé the sense of him- or herself as a member of the profession, encouraging and fostering a self-image as a legitimate member of the community of scholars. (p. 101)

For purposes of this chapter, I think the way one of the interviewees described the term *mentor* serves well as an operational definition. She described a person who fulfills some of Simeone's criteria for sponsorship or mentorship.

> To me, when I think of mentors, I think of an academic conscience. This person is totally unlike me, not what I'd want to be as a teacher. He's what I'd like to be in research and writing, in his scholarly business. He's a real scholar. He always is researching, always writing, always wanting to do the next study. It's almost like he's driven. Sometimes when I don't want to write, I'll go talk to him. He is brutal, no sensitivity to people whatsoever, but just really gives me the kick in the rear that I need. . . . In the past I'd always been attracted to people who have been sensitive and nurturing types. But I keep going back to this person to get slapped down, but I always come back stronger. . . . It's kind of confusing in a way. Mentors should be teachers. I'm not really sure what I'm saying.

In what she erroneously sees as her confusion, she has described well the intricacies that attend academic mentors. Her term *academic conscience* is evocative of what mentoring might mean in its best sense: a model for excellence in the work one has chosen, an individual who helps evoke the best from others. While this particular mentor's rear-kicking style may be inappropriate for many, his models of achievement, of hard work, and of excellence are exemplary.

I asked all participants in my study about their experiences with mentors, if they had had mentors in their work. In most instances, as the discussion ensured, I asked if they themselves had mentored others. Their responses included remarks about mentoring, collaboration, and perceived gender differences in roles and responsibilities.

EXPERIENCING MENTORSHIP

Nearly all interviewees had experience with mentors. Clark (1987) in writing about the relationships between advisers and doctoral students—a common mentor-mentee relationship—implies tyranny or authoritarianism when he notes,

> They [faculty] individually supervise teaching assistants, and auxiliary personnel involved in "their" work. Personal rulership is quite strong in advanced research and teaching; it is certainly found in the supervision of the graduate student or dissertation research. The "mentoring" role of one or two people takes over from the collective responsibility of the department or the institution. (pp. 152–153)

None of the interviewees reported anything resembling Clark's rulership concept or tyranny.

Many of the experiences the faculty had with mentors were the traditional ones of an older person providing help or advice to a younger, usually less experienced person. For male faculty, there were several instances of senior faculty, generally but not always males, urging them to undertake doctoral work, taking them to conferences or on consultation trips, and writing jointly with them. No male indicated that he had not been helped by another faculty member, usually male, in acclimating himself to the professional role.

As Doctoral Students

A retired professor of social studies education remembered his doctoral adviser-mentor fondly. The two eventually became junior and senior faculty members in the same institution.

> He was very much interested in me. I think he had ambitions for me which ultimately came true when I became a department head. But I

don't see that as his original intent; I was just another student among
many. There were returning GIs all over the place. But he took a lot
of interest in everybody. At the same time he was a very tough task-
master; nothing got by him at all. If it wasn't up to his standards, it
didn't go forward. Nothing satisfied him until it was right. He just
didn't give someone a low grade; he gave it back and made them do
it again until they got it right. And that taught me something that
has, in a way, been a burden to me. I never felt that I could give a
student a B-minus on a paper and write a brief comment on it and
just give it back to him. It was just not part of the culture I was developed in. So his mentoring was of the kind that if you're going to be a
teacher, you've got to respect your students as people but you also
have to expect a lot of them. You can't do that kind of teaching if
you don't have high standards for yourself, of what is good scholarship, what is good teaching. To be a good mentor, you have to
model.

This individual's recollections, recorded years after his mentoring experience, reflect what is so potent in mentoring. His mentor had worked with
him in such a manner as to promote high standards, even inculcating a
sense of academic culture, with a joint responsibility between students and
faculty. The mentor was the *academic conscience* much in the spirit of the
earlier observation. Possessed of unusually high standards himself, this
mentor passed on a concern for standards to his mentee who, in turn,
passed it on to his students. His recollections present an ideal picture of a
positive mentoring relationship.

A male professor of foundations at a state university noted that, as
was the case with several interviewees, he had had two mentors:

My professor of social history, he blew me away intellectually; in fact,
much of what I do I owe to him. He was my intellectual mentor; my
professor of curriculum was my teacher education mentor. She
brought me from St. Thomas to St. Maslov. They were very different; they never asked the same questions; they led me in different directions. But they liked each other and helped me. In my prior work
I'd say it was the Jesuits, no particular one, just all those black robes.

Having dual, simultaneous mentors, being pulled in different directions
by two people who want to help—these expressions epitomize one aspect
of academic life, the growth of the inquiring mind. This individual, now a

widely published author in his field, clearly traces much of his success to these two individuals as well as to the black-robed Jesuits.

For a former professor of social studies education, now a dean, the mentor or lodestar of his career was one of his early teachers, as he expressed it, "the best teacher that I ever had."

> He was like a mentor. He was a very outgoing guy; he sometimes would amuse us with songs that always related to the lesson of the day. He began every class with a sign-up sheet and always had a *New Yorker* cartoon on it. That's how I discovered the *New Yorker*. I have been reading it ever since. He was with instruction all the time. And I didn't realize it at the time, but when I became a teacher I was modeling myself on him. I really was.

Among the large number of interviewees who had mentors there were some feelings of unfairness. Some female faculty, when they reported the presence of mentors in their lives, indicated that the initiatives were largely urgings to complete their doctoral work with an occasional goad to publish. Two stated that they had observed that male students received more help from their mentors than females did. No males reported believing that their mentors had taken advantage of them, but two females indicated that they felt they had been exploited. For example, one asserted that she did not get proper and deserved credit for her work in publication by her mentor; another implied that her mentor had used her for his own academic advancement.

A female assistant professor, after commenting on the brevity of the relationship with her doctoral mentor noted:

> Yeah, I had a mentor. Uh, uh . . . in some ways he was real supportive, but I found out later that he was supportive in ways that he wanted me to go, not what I wanted to do. At the time I just didn't key into that. Afterwards, well, you know, I think mentors should be for a long term, not just for doctoral work, but helping you get settled, doing a little collaborative work.

The word *collaborative* stands out in her remarks; it reflects the merging of the terms to which I alluded in the opening section of this chapter. Her experiences as she related them underscore the potential for disappointment and resentment when the relationship either ends or is seen as unfair or dishonest.

A couple of males initially stated that they had not had mentors and then proceeded to describe men who had helped them obtain jobs or graduate assistantships, encouraged them into graduate study, or offered personal advice. Despite questioning them further, I remained uncertain as to exactly what, beyond such matters, these individuals had in mind as the role for mentors. Clearly they had been assisted in some of the ways in which mentors help and support others. The comments of one illustrate the ambiguity they expressed.

> Well, that's a strange thing, yes and no. Yes, in the sense of Professor
> _____ who helped me in the program, helped me get a job. I'm not
> quite sure what he saw in me. Maybe he just needed someone to fill a
> job. I've had a couple of contacts with him since, and I don't con-
> sider him a friend, and I'm sure he doesn't consider me one. He took
> care of his students. But I'm not the sort of person to go looking for
> help, so I guess I didn't have mentors.

One cannot be quite sure whether he experienced mentoring or not, whether he is for whatever reason reluctant to admit that he was men-tored. Two other males expressed the strong-man feeling inherent in the phrasing, "I'm not the sort of person to go looking for help."

A male professor of teacher education at a regional university similarly noted that his experiences with mentors did not fit the current descrip-tions:

> No, not the way we talk about them today. I had people who filled
> the role. In my lifetime I had people who really had an impact on the
> way I think, the way I do things. The first was the county superinten-
> dent under whom I served for four years. He was the one who en-
> couraged me to get a doctorate. He didn't have one but thought I
> could go somewhere if I had one. Then my doctoral adviser was a tre-
> mendous influence on my thinking. Then when I came to work
> here, the dean was a tremendous influence on me. But none of them
> were mentors the way we talk about them today.

Others had clearly helped this individual, but for whatever reason, he like the male above, was reluctant to term them mentors. In other portions of his interview, he comes across somewhat as one who had worked very hard to get where he was, a rugged individualist who persevered. He was like one or two other males in the study who would acknowledge the insights and assistance of others but not undue influence. As another male professor said, "Sure, he [the adviser] helped me, but I did the work." Still another male affirmed that his doctoral dissertation adviser had helped him, but said, "I didn't put a dedication in my dissertation. Why should I? I wrote it; he only critiqued it." A study involving only 34 individuals in hour-long interviews may be too scant to draw gender differences, but I found it interesting that no female in the study described adviser relationships in this manner. Even the two who had become disenchanted with the subsequent behavior of their advisers acknowledged the mentorlike relationship that had existed and the positive results.

A female assistant professor of science education became introspective when she began talking about mentors and herself. She ruminated on the differences in implication between the terms *role models* and *mentors*. She believed that she had worked with both females and males.

> Surprisingly, one of the things they say about mentors and a lot of times they'll call them role models, I like mentor better because role model somehow suggests—it's not true—but it suggests that females have female role models and males have male role models. I found that most of my role models or mentors happen to be males. I guess at the public school level they were female but at the university level they are both male and female.

A female associate professor in special education at a major private university pointed out how her doctoral adviser had guided her and had treated her like a colleague. "I think my adviser served as a mentor. He gave me a lot of opportunities; I was essentially given the opportunity to be a colleague. He was always there to strengthen my research skills." The "opportunity to be a colleague" is an important concept in mentoring in academic life. This faculty member believed that the way her mentor had worked with her had helped her in her subsequent work as a faculty member. "I felt as though I knew what to do when I became a professor." A female assistant professor said of her faculty mentor that he "treated me like an equal." The words *colleague* and *equal* are crucial in relationships in academic life. Without the personal autonomy implicit in both words, mentor-mentee relationship can be detrimental to growth and development, fostering a dependency on the part of the mentee. This potential for dependency may be what makes some people uncomfortable with the mentoring process. Done with respect and dignity, however, as it appears to have been the case in the two previously cited instances, it promotes personal power and autonomy.

A female professor and department chair at a major private university talked about her doctoral adviser in warm terms. "My major adviser was very humane, still is, I shouldn't talk about him as though he were dead. I learned how to work with people from him. No mentors here, though." Uttered in a suddenly dry tone, the expression, "No mentors here, though," was one of frustration. She was like several people in the study who, having experienced the pleasure of working in collaborative ways with mentors, became almost resentful when they could no longer do so.

As Faculty

Only one interviewee experienced an institutional mentoring program in which she was the specific mentoring responsibility of a mentoring senior faculty member. In all other instances in the study, faculty experiences with mentors from their own institutions appear to be largely the result of either serendipity or the initiative of an individual senior faculty member because he or she had taken an interest in a junior faculty member or was convinced that such activity is a professional responsibility.

A female professor of elementary education at a state college had several good experiences in mentoring, especially with two mentors.

> I feel very strongly that I've had mentors, and I was trying to fig-
> ure out why things worked out that way. Did I seek them out,
> did they seek me out? When I started my first job, I mentioned
> that I talked to the school psychologist about my interest in kids
> with problems, and he spent a lot of time telling me to go ahead
> and pursue that advanced degree. When I came here, a person
> who is no longer here—now president of another college—after
> my first year here said to me, "You need to get out to professional
> organizations." So he said, "Go." He had a seat on a policy board
> and that was expiring. He said, "I'd like you to come with me,
> and I'll introduce you and we can sort of pass that seat along." I also
> listened when we had department meetings and talked about people
> up for promotion and tenure. I was really paying attention to the
> whole process. When he was chair, he really encouraged me and
> supported me and saw that I got super merit. He's a real nurtur-
> ing man.

Her second mentor clearly performed multiple roles with and for her. He helped her become known in the important world of professional organizations and associations, and he helped her to learn of the complexities of promotion and tenure. She questioned if there is something in her makeup, her character that leads her to mentoring relationships, thus raising an interesting question. Some people may be innately more drawn to the kinds of personal relationships that mentoring promotes while others are disinclined to participate for personal reasons. Although this study is too narrow in its scope to permit much elaboration on the issue, it is a provocative one that merits further examination.

These faculty members' experiences were dramatically different from that of another female faculty member at another institution. Lacking the kind of faculty mentoring support noted above, she could not get financial support vital to attending meetings.

> I had a paper accepted at AACTE, and the department didn't have any money to send me. It was competitive to get a paper accepted and they still wouldn't send me. I went to the dean to ask for money. It seems to me that they would want me to go—it's the only paper from the college that was accepted. Why wouldn't they want me to present and represent the college?

When asked if she thought she would have gotten money to attend a conference if she had been a male, she responded, "Yes, I really do, honestly believe that. Um, I won't say anymore about that—you already know how I feel about that. It really floored me that they wouldn't let me go. But that's enough of that." This faculty member was one of those who indicated that she had no mentors at her place of work. Whether her belief that her failure to attend the conference because of lack of available funding was truly a gender one is not the point. The point is that she felt powerless to pursue the issue and was disgruntled and unhappy. One wonders if a mentor relationship would have been helpful.

I encountered only one instance of an older faculty member looking to a younger one as a model. One wonders how widespread it could become if individuals were to shed their various biases about age. A male faculty member, an associate professor, indicated that if he currently had a mentor it was a much younger faculty member who impressed him with his energy and his scholarly activity. He indicated that, although there was no formal relationship between the two, he watched the other and learned from him. The younger man had been prepared in a doctoral program that stressed research and scholarship while the older had not. Lawson (1990) indicates that the faculty group he calls the professional scholars have become important on campuses in SCDEs since the 1970s. He notes that, "The professional scholars are an emergent and increasingly powerful group because of the prestige they are perceived to bring to SCDEs and because their work orientations are congruent with those of faculty in colleges of arts and sciences" (p. 61).

SERVING AS MENTORS

Discussions of mentoring with these faculty inevitably led to comments about themselves as mentors. Sometimes I prompted the remarks by asking if they had served as mentors. On other occasions, they themselves began talking about how they had been or were now mentors. Their mentoring was either with doctoral students or with colleagues. Those with experiences mentoring others clearly liked what they had done.

For Doctoral Students

For several faculty, their mentoring of others has come through their work with doctoral students. A male foundations professor commits himself to long-term relationships with his doctoral students:

> The five or six doctoral students I've had over the last years have all been almost intimate friends. They're my best friends. In fact, there is a little group of five or six of us that plan conferences that we go to and based on whether or not we can get together. They call our spare bedroom their home.

A male science education professor, when asked if he had mentored anyone, described his relationship with former students. He noted,

> I would hope so! Some of the students in the past, some of them who got their doctoral degrees, even their master's degrees—I get Christmas cards from them; if they're going through town they say hello. I guess that's mentoring. One of the students was in town last week. She came by and asked about the family and stuff. She told me all about her work. So we're still in touch. I guess you'd call that mentoring.

His relationships with former students appear to have been less intellectual than those of some other faculty, more personal and social. Is this mentoring? He thinks so. I am uncertain, even though his relationships appear to be nurturing and helpful to those entering the professoriate.

A male reading professor indicated that he had helped many doctoral students and had also given them advice on fiscal matters:

> Oh yes, I've had 37 doctoral students and my candidates are not nearly as dollar-hungry as I am. They're a little more research oriented and production of new information oriented; I'm teaching

oriented. But if my students were to say anything that I've told them it would be: amateurs give it away; professionals get paid.

The professor was merely advising his students the same way he had been advised earlier. He indicated that his second mentor, as he described the situation, had urged in a similar manner: "My second mentor trained his people in what you might call 'edubusiness,' he made us entrepreneurs. Nearly everyone of us who studied with him is placed in a college or university somewhere and none of us is poor." His first mentor was a woman who had worked on his academic development. Shortly after he had entered a master's program, she summoned him. "The first one was a lady who had earned her doctorate at 60. Immediately when I got into her course, she did for me what she had done for all her students, made an appointment for an individual conference and she turned me into a student."

A female department chair also cited doctoral students as her outlet for mentoring:

> Oh yes, I have been a mentor for doctoral students. I just got a letter from my first doctoral student last week, in which he thanked me for getting him to do the things he has to do now that he is a faculty member. I always try to give doctoral students the opportunities to meet people in the field; I always see to it that they go to national conventions. It's always exciting for them to meet people who have written things, and I know so many of them. I encourage them to begin their writing, to publish from their dissertations. I've done presentations with them and, yes, I've written with them.

This faculty member gave no indication of having been mentored during her graduate studies. But she was clearly giving to students what she had lacked in her own work. It appears that she is fulfilling the mentoring function in an ideal way: indications of help but none of control or domination.

Another female faculty member who had had no mentoring assistance in her graduate work, when asked if she was now mentoring students, replied in a somewhat surprised tone, "Why, no, I haven't."

For Other Faculty

One male professor I interviewed was at a university with a formal mentoring program. The provost, apparently convinced that the rigorous pressures necessary for promotion and tenure were growing ever more difficult for junior faculty, developed a formal, mandatory structure linking senior faculty members with junior faculty members. The senior faculty member was intensely excited with his experiences in mentoring a junior faculty member.

> The provost has insisted on a mentoring program for new faculty members because he wants to make sure that they are successful in terms of publications and research and successful in teaching, that they don't get lost in the thing. I talk to her about the whole thing. I don't mean I've lectured her, but I tell her about the expectation of what we are doing, the past history, the problems. Reassure her about her class outlines, a lot of reassurance. Reassure her, hell, when you get back 30 class evaluations and five of them say that you're not worth dung, 20 others are good, what do you do, how do you feel about it? Go out and have a drink with some students. There are real important things in that sort of relationship. I just love mentoring. I just absolutely love it. I suspect this is probably what I like best.

Occasionally a faculty member served as a mentor for an individual at another institution. Asked if he had ever served as a mentor for others, a male faculty member replied,

> Yes, once with a woman who was working at another institution; she'd called and asked me if I would read some of her stuff. I did and we've talked together five or six times since; we always spend a half hour together at AERA. We've exchanged papers several times.

This relationship may be model for the future as technology makes it easier for mentors and mentees to communicate from one campus to another. The various computer networks may greatly augment the mentoring process.

MENTORS AS COLLEAGUES

Mentoring is inherently an implied close personal relationship between two individuals; and faculty often joined their remarks about mentoring with observations about collaboration, another relationship implying closeness, an opportunity for growth and development. Some faculty believed that they functioned more effectively when working collaboratively with others. Faculty development programs at some institutions include opportunities for both mentoring and collaboration. Several faculty in this study indicated that they had collaborated in scholarly activities with their mentors. The two concepts of mentoring and collaboration clearly merge in some useful ways.

Female faculty in this study occasionally saw other females who were serving in a mentoring capacity as colleagues. An assistant professor spoke of how, after she had been mentored by two male faculty, she met someone who, even though she served as her doctoral adviser, became a colleague with whom she still works.

> Then she came along and served as my mentor since then. It's more of a colleague. I can remember when she looked at my first draft of my first couple of chapters of my dissertation; there was this red ink everywhere. I looked at it and I said, no one has done this before. My writing is good; no one had picked on my writing before. But she did it. She worked with me all year and we got it finished.

Inasmuch as she had worked with mentors of both genders, I asked her which she was more comfortable with, a male or female mentor. She replied, "Much more with the woman. The further I've gotten involved with higher education, the more I've had nasty experiences with men."

A female assistant professor in a southern state university similarly believes that gender gets in the way of developing relationships, particularly with males. Consequently, the potential pool of mentors for her is diminished. "My gender gets in the way. It just seems that I'm not able to work cooperatively with males. I haven't been able to do that much. . . . I'm hesitant because I haven't really worked much with men. It starts out cooperatively but then it gets competitive."

A female assistant professor of teacher education was the only person who emphatically stated that she had never had any mentors; further, she contended that there were no mentoring activities where she was working. She clearly would like some.

> Lack of mentors? Yes, I do lack them. I never had any. I don't know why they don't mentor here, do collaborative research. It would make success more likely. It seems to me that you hire people to be successful. And even when you come up here. There's very much a male role model, male orientation model here.

She believed that her lack of mentoring relationship was at least in part a function of the "male orientation model" in her institution. Like the

faculty member who thought she might have gotten to go to the conference if she had been male, this faculty member believes that there is gender
discrimination or differentiation. Whether or not the belief accurately reflects the reality is not the point; the point is that she believes it and the
belief appears to inhibit relationships.

CONCLUSION

Mentoring may exist for several reasons, but the most critical are the
professional and personal development of faculty. The males in this study
clearly had many opportunities to grow and develop under the sponsorship and support of mentors. Further, their careers were continually en-
hanced by numbers of mentorlike colleagues. They were helped to get
their work published; they were occasionally invited to participate in lucra-
tive consultation ventures.

The females in the study, to be sure, were not bereft or mentor-
collaborator relationships, but the relationships were less frequent and less
intense. Some had none of any substance. One cannot on the basis of
these interviews establish either the degree to which the situation is widespread or the cause of the different situations. But one can suggest that
conditions for mentoring are not equal for males and females, that there
are gender issues in the academic workplace that inhibit the development
of females and appear to promote that of males. In Chapter 6 I will
examine in more detail additional aspects of the gender issues in the teacher
education professoriate.

6 Satisfactions and Frustrations

I wouldn't change my life for anything.

— *Male full professor*

Someday I'm going to speak out. It might not make any difference but it would make me feel better.

— *Female associate professor*

As I was reflecting and questioning while attempting to make sense of all the material I had gathered, I received a note from one of the female participants in the study, who wrote, "I'm looking forward to reading it [the book]. I was promoted to professor this past year. My work is exciting and fulfilling!" In her interview she had noted that "Oh, I like to be contributing, writing. I'm excited about my future." Her work continues to be exciting; her note had the same sense of joy in her work and life that characterized her interview.

Perhaps as is the case in nearly all lives, the lives of these faculty are very complex. Rarely is anything purely a satisfaction or a frustration. Their satisfactions and frustrations comingle. One notes, for example, that satisfaction in teaching students is related to a frustration in being unable to write and conduct research because of excessive time demands.

POSITIVE ATTITUDES

"Exciting and fulfilling." The words bespeak a quality of life that generally runs through the remarks of all the interviewees. In Terkel's (1974) *Working*, his respondents give witness to the importance of work in modern society, how our work and how others view it partially defines

85

us. For many of the individuals he interviewed, positive feelings about themselves and their work were important.

Faculty in this study think well of their work. A female assistant professor noted, "I think the satisfaction now is in the coordination of the faculty, the sense of working together. The fact that I have a lot of autonomy is very satisfying." Phrases such as "a good place to be," "pleasant colleagues," "the stimulation of ideas" permeated the interviewee remarks. There was little of a fortress mentality, of a defensiveness about these faculty and their place in higher education. They are examples of those who Wisniewski and I (1989a) describe as having thrived.

The positive faculty attitudes reinforce the conclusions of the RATE studies over the last six years, which have demonstrated that teacher-education faculty and students throughout the country perceive their preparation programs very positively. Howey has consistently found that teacher educators are favorably disposed about their work. In 1989, he pointed out how teacher-education faculty are positive about their students, their teaching, and their work, a point supported in the study he and Zimpher (1989) conducted in a number of institutions. Yet Howey (1982) also observes that "People in teacher education are being asked to accomplish more with fewer resources and with less to say about the directions being charted for how teachers will be prepared" (p. 3).

But sometimes the faculty perceive that others think ill of them and their work. All are not content with how others view them. A female full professor reflected a perennial view when she commented, "I really like what I do, but I get frustrated in the university setting over the lack of respect for education; I'm not real happy with the arts and sciences attitude toward us." Still she expressed satisfaction with her life and her work. A male associate professor felt that teacher educators do not have as much control over their programs as he would like. "Our biggest problem is that the nonschool people control the college; we are being dominated by their organizations. The counseling people with APA [American Psychological Association]. So teacher education is left behind; the others luxuriate in their situation." Thus a few teacher education faculty sense that some others external to their SCDEs may not respect them, while there also exists a worry that even within the SCDEs there are groups of faculty who have more power than they do.

But these faculty nonetheless feel positively about their work. Such may be the case because conditions in teacher education were never much different from Howey's description, and teacher educators have remained positive through adversity. Or, these teacher educators may be an unusually optimistic group; they remain confident and upbeat despite whatever else may be going on. At the close of his interview, a senior male faculty member noted, "Deep down I feel very positive. I wouldn't change my life for anything. After I retire I might want to be an anthropologist, but this is a good life." There are numerous satisfactions to the good professional life in higher education, one of which is the work that faculty do with students.

Fondness for Students

When asked what the major satisfactions were with their work, the interviewees very often mentioned their students as the prime sources of satisfaction. In this respect they closely resemble their earlier selves when they were lower-school teachers. They echo what Lortie (1975) demonstrated in his study, namely that the primary source of satisfaction for teachers is working with students. Given the extensive backgrounds in public education possessed by the individuals in my study, it comes as no surprise to learn that they rate their work with students so highly. Many of them are, after all, first and foremost, teachers.

A female associate professor finds enjoyment in observing the growth of students as they move through the professional sequence.

> I suppose the greatest satisfaction I get is that we are able to watch a group go from beginning their programs all the way through to the finish, to their student teaching. My greatest satisfaction is being able to watch that person develop from not being sure of herself into being a polished, well, they might not be polished or too confident, but when they're in student teaching, I get to see how they have developed.

It is interesting to note that she exercises such care in observing growth and takes such joy in it, while being realistic enough to suggest that even though her students grow they lack some polish and confidence.

A female professor of social studies education also gets her primary satisfaction from her work with students and particularly enjoys the variety of student levels with which she works. "I enjoy the students at all levels. I teach all levels, undergraduates and graduates. I teach the doctoral seminar and that gives me an opportunity to meet all the graduate students." She is, of course, also gaining satisfaction from watching the development of students. She is doing so by watching and working with students at various developmental levels at the same time, while the previous faculty member enjoys watching individual students develop over the continuum of a couple of years. One recalls how similar in kind this feeling about watching students develop is to the almost cliché response of lower-school teachers when asked what they like about teaching. The answer often comes out in some form of how they like to see the children grow and mature; they like the proverbial light that goes on when students suddenly appear to have grasped some concept. This fondness for human growth and development may be the bind that, in fact, joins teachers at all levels. It is certainly present in these faculty to a very high degree.

Seeing students as the primary source of satisfaction was not gender specific, even though females were more likely to discuss it than males, some of whom also cited their work with students as their basic source of satisfaction. A male reading professor found pleasure in both teaching the students and in following their careers.

> My greatest satisfaction over the years has been the students I've worked with. We don't have—in this department—undergraduate advisees but I've taught undergraduates and recruited many of them into our master's program and even into the doctoral program. And it's always a thrill to see how well they're doing. [Goes to a shelf and takes down two pictures.] Here are two of them. The lady is even older than I am. She's a Title I teacher; the male is an assistant professor of reading. They both stay in touch.

I have rarely been as moved in my many conversations with professors of education both in this study and in other contexts as I was at this moment, when this distinguished professor of reading took the two pictures of his former students in hand and spoke about them. The pride he took in them was so evident. There were other pictures of former students on the shelf as well. His pictures were the objective correlative of the students he and other faculty talked about so enthusiastically.

A male science educator takes similar satisfaction in hearing from and staying in touch with former students. His remarks reveal that what they do reflects on his own sense of self. Perhaps like many teachers, he finds joy in the accomplishments of those whom he has taught and lives a bit vicariously in their lives. He finds meaning in his own life from the work of his former students. "My chief satisfactions are talking with former students I've had about what they're doing and reflecting on the fact that I've taught them. In part, it reflects on some of the things I've done."

A female science educator similarly enjoys her teaching and also likes to hear from students that they have learned much from her and admire her.

> I get a lot of satisfaction in working with the students. When they come back and say, "I was just telling my husband or my mother or

someone that I want to be just like Dr. _____. I like the way she does this or that." That's satisfying. It gives meaning to the daily work that we do.

Praise for Students

These faculty not only enjoy working with students; they also praise them highly. They are proud of them. A male professor of foundations expressed his belief in students, in their role as future teachers.

I spend a lot of time thinking about this. The age thing is overwhelming; what they don't know is stunning. But if someone said to me that someone is going to die and you can leave them in the care of a group as death comes, who would it be. I'd pick elementary and secondary teachers, my former students. As a people, I'd have more trust in them than any other group. The ones going into teaching are profoundly trustworthy, very worried about hurting someone else.

When I asked how teacher education students of today compare with those of a decade ago, they indicated that they were very impressed with today's students. Faculty were nearly universal in their praise of students, generally arguing that today's students in teacher preparation were better academically than students in the past, an interesting contention given what is more typically said about students in teacher preparation. The national press and numerous reports have in the past decade lambasted teacher education and its students for the alleged low level of academic potential and performance. Yet these individual faculty do not feel negative about their students; they believe that their students are extremely capable. Is this view defensiveness? It would appear not to be so from the texts of their observations.

A female associate professor indicated that she believed that the students are better, and that preparation programs for them are better as well. "My feeling is that the students are better. I also think that we know more about the practice of things like direct instruction, a structured body of knowledge. There's more substance to the teacher-education literature and we're getting better students."

A male professor believes they are much better than a few years ago; he also contends that the supervising teachers are better.

I don't think there is any comparison. I think people going out now are ready from the first day to teach. Why do I think they're better prepared? We know a lot more than we used to. The whole field experiences early on in their time here. When they go into student teaching, they are much better prepared; they can take over their own class much sooner. The supervising teachers are better. The people we thought were good 10, 20 years ago, we wouldn't let our kids near them now. And that first year of internship is very valuable to them. I don't think there's a comparison.

The issue of additional substance in the teacher education curriculum was important for several individuals. The 1980s were marked by much discussion in the teacher-education profession about such matters as a knowledge base for teacher education; the National Council for the Accreditation of Teacher Education has made it paramount in its procedures and requirements. There is a general belief that the knowledge base for teacher education is improving; at the same time, there is contempt expressed by some faculty for what they see as pretentious phrasing. One of the more iconoclastic interviewees observed, "It's what the AACTE people call the knowledge-base part of teaching. God, I hate that term; I think there is a subject matter of what teacher do, but it's not a knowledge base." Yet, irrespective of where these faculty stood on the issue of the knowledge base writ large, they were convinced that more is now known about how learners learn, about how some things are best taught. There was a sense of pride with which these faculty said things such as, "We know more now." Thus they value both their students and their curricula. And they very much want the graduates from their programs to be knowledgeable and skillful.

A male professor of teacher education waxed enthusiastically. A person who divides his time between field work and campus work, he noted both the students' academic achievement and their skill in pedagogy.

> Oh, I rate them higher, much higher in terms of achievement, but also in terms of their teaching. I see more A's in student teaching. I find I'm giving more A's. Last week I saw some beginning teachers who had graduated just last spring. Oh, some of them were good. I hope we don't take too much credit for making them good. They didn't know they were good; they just had it. And we didn't give it to them.

One notes in his remarks two of the many appealing characteristics of these individuals: a sense of pride in the accomplishment of their students and a lack of hubris about their own efforts.

A female science educator was ready to give a guarantee or warranty that today's students were going to become good teachers. She believed that the students preparing in science education were superb. "Academically, we have very good students. And as far as their being prepared, I would vouch for 95% of them coming out as being good teachers."

A male foundations professor found no fault with student intellectual ability; in fact, he found students, "Fine, just fine." But he worried about their lack of a social conscience and the presence of self-interest. He also indicated that he might be wanting to see in them what he wanted to see in himself.

> Fifteen years ago, undergraduates were a lot more concerned
> with the things foundations professors care about, the social is-
> sues. For political motivations, they saw social and cultural bias
> and were a lot more motivated to fight for the underdog. And
> you know, now you can't even talk about that in front of under-
> graduates. Maybe it's beginning to change a little bit; I don't
> know.

This faculty member may have been responding to the general lack of social concerns that characterized college students in the late 1980s. He may also have discerned the beginnings of a trend that is now apparently gaining some momentum, namely, a growing social awareness on the part of some students. His worry is a critical one for the profession: the social values of its graduates who enter teaching. As was clear in Chapter 1, these faculty entered teaching with a set of values, however haphazardly they might have chosen the profession. A few worry about the values of the current cohorts of students.

A male science educator expressed one of the few negative views about recent students; he was concerned with what he perceived as an inability of his current elementary education students to problem solve.

> In elementary, when I look back on what I was doing 10 years ago
> and what I do now, there has been a tremendous drop in the level of
> difficulty. I'd go back to what a high-school teacher said to me. I told
> them that they're scared to think, and he told me that I was getting
> the problems he had been dealing with. The reason you don't see it
> in secondary is because they choose science as major, but in early
> childhood, they don't know what they want to do; it's a problem
> when they can get a degree without knowing much science. It was
> much better 10 years ago; you'd give them a problem and they could
> think it through.

Joy in Teaching

For some the major satisfaction comes from the teaching. Occasionally it appeared that teaching is the only totally sane thing in their lives, the one thing over which they believe they have total control. Despite the protestations of the greater freedom in higher education compared with life in the lower schools cited in Chapter 2, total freedom is not available to many. Teaching provides a major vehicle for freedom, freedom of expression, of choice of materials, of pedagogy. "Here I have the freedom to do what I choose in my teaching."

A male associate professor of elementary education luxuriates in the academic freedom his teaching provides. "I've felt free to teach the way I want to teach, including the content I want to include, to develop a course I want to develop, to do the sorts of things that I want to do. That's what's a real source of satisfaction around here." His phrase "a real source of satisfaction around here" suggests that he believes that his colleagues share the joy in teaching and the freedom that accompanies it at this institution.

For a female assistant professor in special education teaching is a primary source of self-assurance and sense of belonging. She notes, "Right now my chief satisfaction comes from my teaching. It is the one time—actually four times a week times three—when I really know what I'm doing. The students are good; they work hard." Her 12 hours of teaching provide her with a clear sense of accomplishment, as she has the opportunity to be with those students who "work hard." Of course, she also pointed out that the 12 hours of teaching made accomplishing the other things in research and scholarship more difficult than if she had a lower teaching load. It is worth noting that she teaches a 12-hour load each semester, three more than the male professor of foundations who pointed out that teaching only nine hours was one of the reasons that he published a great deal: "You are teaching nine hours a week. What do you do if you don't do it?" Joy in teaching for this female assistant professor might be even higher if she taught fewer hours.

A male professor of teacher education finds joy in working with students when they are in the field doing their student teaching or interning. For some he might appear to be an anomaly: a male full professor who enjoys working with student teachers. The RATE studies, for example, show that full professors of both genders do less supervision of student teachers than other faculty and that *male* full professors do even less. Yet he observes, "I get some of my biggest enjoyment in working with interns and student teachers. This semester I've got three credits in student teaching. I just feel that if I ever do any good, that's where I'll do it. I have a seminar I teach graduate students. I like the give-and-take of that; we talk about ideas." In his remarks he combines the sources of pleasure many describe: watching students mature in their professional work in the field and being able to teach them in seminar and watch the ideas ebb and flow.

A male foundations professor similarly finds teaching his greatest joy but is not pleased with the environment in which he must teach. He laments that teaching must be done in institutions; he would prefer to be teaching in nonschool settings, places not constricted by the restraints that organizations and institutions impose. Nonetheless he finds joy in the life of the professor doing his teaching.

> The greatest satisfaction is teaching, but not to have to do it in a hole like this. The tragedy is that if you're committed to teaching, you have to do it in an institution. That's just the way it is. I've developed a sense of the sacredness of teacher-student transactions. I still think the professional life is great. The life in professional schools is very good. The idea of praxis, the continual assault of ideas is what keeps me going.

FRUSTRATIONS

In the midst of all that is good and empowering about being faculty members in higher education lie frustrations as well. Those who work in higher education know that it is a life of intermingled satisfaction and frustration. Sometimes the very things that bring pleasure can bring disappointment, for as the foundations professor noted above, teaching is a great source of satisfaction, but the conditions under which faculty sometimes teach can be a source of frustration.

Sense of Impotence

Even teaching the students can sometimes be frustrating. A female educator noted that students cause her heartache. "The thing that causes me the most heartache is when I really try hard and what I give to students is rejected in terms of trying to get them to do something in their own student teaching other than lecture, trying to get them to do more activities with the students, involve them with the lessons." Her experience and comments echo my own earlier remarks about the struggle for student teachers' souls in the lower schools.

> In many instances, higher-education faculty and the lower-school teachers vie for the soul of the student teacher. Generally it is no contest. The veteran

teacher, often replete with answers and work sheets to solve, putatively, every problem, wins allegiance. Quickly, the familiar Ivory Tower-Real World clash arises, and the university faculty member becomes the "distracting" voice of novelty, experimentation, and learning theory in the chorus of pragmatism. (Ducharme, 1986b, p. 53)

This lack of application by students of what one has taught them combined with the students' total embrace of the pragmatism of the field can be enormously frustrating, particularly for individuals who derive primary satisfaction from working with students. The situation, after all, is one of rejection, a condition that few individuals enjoy. One need not delve very deeply into psychological motivations of ourselves as faculty to discern certain parent-child aspects of the faculty-student relationships, and few parents enjoy rejection of values and norms of behavior. Such is particularly the case in a situation such as this when the new source of wisdom or role model for the student may be one who has faulted higher education and its faculty and programs.

Dissatisfaction with Self

A female associate professor finds frustration both in her performance at national conferences and at the general scholarly level at some conferences. She, like so many others in teaching, aims for perfection and is frustrated when she falls short.

> I'm frustrated by national conferences in that I always come away feeling that I didn't present the way I teach. I lecture and I'm not sure I have to in order to get it all in. I always wish that I hadn't. That's my greatest source of frustration. And to be real honest with you, I'm not sure I learn much at conferences. Some of the presentations are so unscholarly at some conferences.

It is clear that while she faults her own performances at national conferences, she thinks that others come up shy of excellence as well.

Other faculty frustrations with self included displeasure over the amount of publishing one had done, the type of scholarly work one had engaged in, and the inability to use one's time effectively.

Lack of Time and Conflicting Demands

A male professor of teacher education is frustrated by the lack of time available in the days and weeks to do the things he wants to do. "The biggest frustration is that there are not enough hours in the day to do what I want to do. And I guess that I resent someone dropping a mandate on me saying you will do this or telling me that I will do something I was planning to do anyway." In contrast to some of the comments in Chapter 2, in which the interviewees extoll the freedom of time in higher education, this man finds too little of it, and he clearly believes that on occasion others tell him what to do. He likes neither situation. Time is the major frustration for another male faculty member who complains, "The frustration is not having the time to do the things I want to do. The rules of the game of higher education get in the way of what I want to do. I have a folder at home of things to do, things that will be a contribution to the field, and I just don't have the time."

While one can nod appreciatively at the complaints of lack of time, one also notes that lack of time is a perennial complaint of many individuals in this modern age. One speculates about what might be the level of productivity if institutions gave more time for research and scholarship and demanded less teaching. The RATE studies suggest that while faculty in doctoral level institutions generally teach somewhat less and publish somewhat more than faculty in master's level institutions, the differences in publishing levels are not startling. One cannot conclude whether the modest overall increase in scholarly productivity of faculty in doctoral level institutions is primarily a function of more available time, or a function of who chooses to work in what kinds of institutions, or the nature of the individuals in different institutions. It may be, for example, that faculty in doctoral level institutions who publish frequently would do so irrespective of where they work and of minor differences in teaching responsibilities. Certainly, my own experience as a university department chairperson suggests that faculty with similar assignments will produce sometimes quite different publication results.

Gender Differences in Job Demands

When I visit a teacher preparation program as part of an NCATE team or in any other capacity, I observe men and women working together in apparent harmony. I notice the nearly always higher percentage of men on the faculty, whether the program is preparing elementary or secondary teachers, as well as the higher frequency of male chairpersons. My interviews for this study reveal that beneath the apparent harmony lie some disturbing aspects. A female assistant professor feels frustrated in her attempts to understand higher education and thrive in it. She does not even understand the "rules of the game of higher education" cited by the previous faculty member above.

The whole combination of background and experience was confusing. I felt like I knew the system in the public schools very well. The worst thing for me is that I've been here a year and a half and I still don't know how the system works. It's very confusing. Committee work, areas of investigation, territoriality. The people are all very bright, very intelligent, basically all achievement oriented. How do you break into that? Rank and tenure. Graduate faculty. What does it mean? Who wants it? There's the whole enculturation, the whole system that at least in my doctoral work they didn't teach me anything about it.

Clearly, higher education has not met all of her needs. Her comments echo some of Aisenberg and Harrington's observations from their interviews of women in academic life. For example, they observe,

> Another form of subsidy that women notoriously lack is professional counseling—guidance and instruction in the actual rules of the game. And here our interviews amply bear out the virtual truism that women suffer chronically from lack of professional mentors—that little time is spent by graduate school professors on the careful professional counseling of women. . . . The result for many women is that, on receiving the doctorate, they have little clear idea of how to plan a professional life. (p. 45)

The interviewees used the phrase "rules of the game" several times. The rules are clearly very important as individuals attempt to understand and work and grow within an organization. The kinds of assistance and direction giving that mentors can provide, as I described in Chapter 5, can be critical in a successful career in higher education, but first one must understand what the rules are. Some faculty do not; typically, they are women.

A female professor of science education at a state college expressed puzzlement over what she perceived as differential treatment between men and women. Her remarks were not said in a bitter or confrontational manner, but more in a questioning tone.

> I'm wondering if why I didn't get help in learning what it takes
> to succeed in higher education was because I'm a woman. The
> graduate program I was in was an NSF Institute. I'm wondering
> if the men that went through the program were inducted differ-
> ently; you know, in terms of the informal kind of interactions that
> help one to succeed in a different way than I was. . . . No one told
> me that the *Chronicle of Higher Education* was the place to look for a
> job. I'd been looking in the back pages of the science magazines,

which of course is mostly science jobs, and maybe some science education jobs once a year. So the little things like that I had to learn for
myself.

For this faculty member, part of the academic world was a puzzle that she
might have put together more quickly and more easily with the help of a
mentor. Another female, an assistant professor, is uncertain about who
gets promoted and why.

I really don't know. To some extent, I base that on cases I've known.
But it's so unclear. I know in a couple of instances where they have
been granted tenure, and I was somewhat amazed. I know a couple
of other instances where they have not been granted tenure, and I
was shocked.

For another female faculty member, there may be an inherent gender
wall that for some, precludes mentoring and collaborating.

I have two other colleagues I work with. I'm beginning to know two
or three male faculty members. And it's becoming pretty clear that
there is no interaction. You know, there's the courtesy stuff. They
talk and then they go and do whatever it is they are doing. Actually,
I'm beginning to think male faculty, they're basically passive-
aggressive. After they talk with you, they go off and do what they
please.

This faculty member has experienced what Simeone (1987) described
when she wrote,

A sense of isolation and difference pervades the histories of women of achievement in traditionally male arenas. There are few women in comparable situations, and while an individual woman may see herself as simply another
member of the group, her male colleagues are likely to perceive her as being
quite different from themselves. This perception of difference, often coupled
with denigrating attitudes if not indeed caused by them, results in women's
exclusion from the truly meaningful and important interactions with male
colleagues and superiors. (p. 77)

Of course, limited studies such as this do not gather the adequate number
of respondents to determine the degree to which the feelings are general-
ized across institutions. Nor do they permit an expanded examination of
whether the conditions can be effectively ameliorated or not. It is difficult
to imagine a truly honest environment with the views expressed in this

section remaining unspoken and unacknowledged. It is equally difficult to imagine them being expressed openly because of conditioning, fear of recrimination, or some other causes. One does not say, "Someday I'm going to speak out" without having harbored thought of having been ill treated for a long time. Others expressed related views.

A tenured female associate professor in a department with six males, three of whom are full professors, and ten females, none of whom is a full professor, believes that the workload is disproportionately distributed.

> Well, I think it's general, well, I don't know generally, but specifi-
> cally—I know in our department that women are the work horses.
> They do the heavy teaching, they do the heavy supervision. They
> care about supervision, and I really think there's a subtle sex discrimi-
> nation. I haven't had the courage yet to talk about it. There's a little
> subtlety like, at a faculty meeting, a male can come up with an idea
> and two years later it's still being called the [man's name] idea. A wom-
> an can come up with an idea and everybody forgets it. A man can
> say the same thing and get credit for the idea. It's just subtle little
> things, the merit pay kind of thing and what's expected. Or when
> one of our secretaries is leaving, the female faculty members are al-
> ways expected to plan the luncheon. If there's expected to be some-
> one to supervise a student organization, that sort of thing, a female is
> expected to be the supervisor. I am supervising 20 student teachers
> this semester, and a male colleague across the hall is supervising three,
> and we are getting the same amount of credit. I'm supervising 20 and
> he's supervising three! This has happened year after year after year.
> That's not atypical. The other person who has as many student teach-
> ers as I have is also a female. And we're expected to get our work
> done, and do research and writing and do everything else. For men it
> seems like doors are opened for them and things pushed out of their
> way so that they can write and do their research. People help them.
> We're supposed to do all these things and do research. It's such a
> touchy issue. If you just mention sexual discrimination, people say,
> "Oh God, I'm so tired of talking about that! We've been talking
> about it for years!" That's one reason I'm reluctant to say anything
> about it.

The uncertainty of not knowing what the rules are, of being or feeling overloaded with tasks, the perceived disproportionate assignments of du-ties can lead to a variety of reactions, none of them healthy. Not being certain who is making the decisions and under what possibly hidden criteria can lead to near paranoia. One female faculty member finds the situations threatening and uncomfortable. She is careful of her words and actions. Her remarks suggest an almost Kafkasque quality to part of her life.

> You don't want to offend anyone. You know, when the time comes
> around to vote for promotion or tenure, if you've offended someone
> without even knowing it, that can be bad. That's scarier to me than
> the list of things I'm supposed to do. So I'm worried about whose
> toes I may be stepping on.

For some, it is possible in the house of higher education to offend without knowing, a consequence of which can be or is believed can be, a failure to gain tenure or promotion. Glass ceilings come in a variety of colors and shapes, not always discernible, but always threatening.

Remarks of frustration with what for some is a male-dominated professional world were not limited to assistant and associate professors. A female full professor and department chair expressed extreme frustration with some of the rules of the game, only this game was in the broader world of the university at large beyond the SCDE. Discomfort exists even at the top of the status level of full professor.

> The other thing that is frustrating is the committee work and the way
> women are treated. I get disgusted by the number of meetings that I
> go to where I may be the only woman in the meeting and people
> don't listen to what I have to say in the conversation. You learn to
> deal with it, even in the senate. It's just ridiculous. There are only
> three women professors in the whole college. In salaries, I know that
> I'm behind men who are full professors.

Her remarks about not being listened to echo those of the female associate professor cited earlier in this chapter who noted, "A woman can come up with an idea and everybody forgets it."

Differentiated Work

A number of studies, most particularly the RATE studies, have shown that female faculty have heavier advising, supervising, and teaching loads than do male faculty. As Kluender and I (1990) point out, "Women do more field supervision and more teaching. Therefore, women may publish less because they are often asked to assume supervisory responsibilities at a disproportionate level, and they teach more" (p. 47). For some faculty this can become oppressive. One female faculty member cited the number of advisees she had, and the difficulties that inhere in not doing the advising the way she thinks she should do it.

> I have 110 advisees. Yeah, I've been told to shut the door and do my writing. Maybe it's my elementary school background, but I just can't do that. Maybe I need to learn to be a little more selfish. That's all I know; ask me another day, and maybe you might hear something different.

Her tone throughout most of the interview was very positive. At this time, however, there was a kind of whimsical tone that slowly wound down into the "ask me another day" mood, one that suggests both perplexity and resignation. She is torn between meeting what she perceives to be student needs and her need to write and publish. The student needs win out. The male faculty members advise her to close her door and do her writing, but they do not volunteer to help her with the work for which she feels responsible. A Catch-22 situation.

For another female faculty member, the demands made on her by female students were frustrating. She expressed concern that elementary preparation students feel condescended to by male faculty in their classes.

> I think what else is frustrating to me is the students, the young women students I have. I feel I'm running a home for our younger sisters. They feel they've experienced this sense of not being good enough academically in class—these are elementary education majors and they feel the male faculty don't think much of them.

She also made these comments dispassionately. Of course, they reveal more frustration with the male faculty perceived treatment of female elementary preparation students than they do with the students. They also reveal some sense of frustration that as a woman she, like the last woman whom I quoted, feels obligated to respond to their needs. The comment about the students feeling that male faculty see them as not good academically recalls the earlier remark of the male faculty member who believed that today's elementary education students—chiefly female—are not good at problem solving. Is it possible not to convey such views to students?

Her observations regarding the "home for our younger sisters" echo my personal experiences from 19 years of work as a university department chairperson, namely, that females are in the minority on faculty rosters but in the majority on teacher education student rosters. As a consequence of this numerical condition and a rise in the importance and visibility of women's issues on campuses, female faculty do a disproportionate amount of advising. Increasingly, there is a legitimate desire to have female faculty on all doctoral committees of female candidates, to have females advising females. Further, as one interviewee pointed out, "Every college committee has to have a woman on it, and I'm usually the one." These conditions contribute to substantial inequities in the work load.

CONCLUSION

It would be easy to dismiss the negative observations about faculty life as occasional misgivings in a very positive environment. It would also be inappropriate. While it is true that these interviews reveal high levels of satisfaction with life and work, the profession should note and react to the negative perceptions. The teacher-education professoriate, after all, exists to prepare the teachers for the nation's schools; a large majority of the students are females. It ill suits the profession to have the female faculty role models for these prospective teachers feeling unfairly treated or being unfairly untreated in work load, salary, rank, and tenure.

Despite the negative aspects of the frustration in the work that I have noted, I return to the "exciting and fulfilling" note with which I opened the chapter. The work *is* good and the faculty find immense fulfillment in it. I recall my intense enjoyment in conducting the interviews for the study and note that the enjoyment came in part from talking with individuals who were positive and affirming about their lives and their work. And these feelings were present across the various ages and in the different levels of experience within higher education.

These are individuals whose feelings of satisfaction far outweigh their feelings of frustration, people with a zest for the professional life. But one *must* attend to the frustrations, particularly to those that bespeak inequities in the professional life.

7 Summing Up

But being a professor is a good life. There is so much diversity. My days are so exciting.

— *Female assistant professor*

I open this final chapter with a quotation from a young female assistant professor exuding excitement in the professional life, for it is the excitement in their lives that has most characterized the words of the faculty. I do so because after some summarizing and reflecting, that is where this story will end: with the excitement of the professional life. The quotation is particularly apt, given its source. For it is the young professors, male and female, who will inherit the professoriate that I have attempted to describe in limited ways. And if the voices in this study have validity, and if the RATE data suggesting larger percentages of females preparing for the professoriate are right, they will be much more in the forefront of leadership in the coming decades. But much must occur before that day comes.

As I neared the end of my verbal journey with the faculty whom I had interviewed, I speculated about the meaning of all the words, the conversations, the feelings. What had I learned? What difference might it make? In this concluding chapter, I will draw some reflective conclusions from the many observations and responses that I have gathered, indicate several connections to the current situation in teacher education, and offer suggestions for further, needed work. But first I will indicate how not all of my questions drew interesting responses and suggest why.

WEAK QUESTIONS

Not all questions in interviews elicit provocative responses. Sometimes what appears to be of momentous significance to someone in the external world is of little moment to those doing the work. Thus I had prepared, partly in conjunction with knowledgeable colleagues, a few questions, that despite my careful preparations, failed to garner rich responses. However, it might be instructive to cite some of the responses and to speculate on the possible reasons for the paucity of the responses.

Perceptions of Colleagues

Among the several questions that elicited little response beyond banalities or vague affirmation was, "How do you regard your colleagues within your academic unit with respect to their overall effectiveness as faculty members?" Individuals generally did not respond with much detail; they simply stated that they thought their colleagues were marvelous or good or okay, with virtually nothing to illustrate or buttress their point of view.

Although there was an occasional distinction drawn between veteran and more recently hired faculty with respect to their preparation for and inclination to do scholarly work, even these comments contained almost no negative or analytic observations. In fact, youthful faculty members respected those more experienced faculty who had done extensive teaching and field work prior to the emergence of scholarly norms for nearly everyone, even though they themselves did not want to do extensive field work. The experienced faculty spoke positively about the younger faculty and their bent toward scholarship and research, even worrying about the expectations being made of them. But in general, the faculty had little to say about their colleagues. People might, in fact, rather talk about themselves than others. I note in reviewing the transcripts that I paid increasingly less attention to the question in later interviews as it repeatedly elicited virtually nothing but bland responses such as, "I like my colleagues," "They're good people, unpretentious," and similar generalizations.

There was a lack of criticism of colleagues beyond the previously noted gender differences in promotion, tenure, and other rewards, or of any specific positive statements. Yet these are not, in reality, criticisms of other faculty as much as criticisms of the system in which they work. I wondered why there is such a lack of criticism. Is it that teacher education faculty are so positively disposed toward one another that true harmony exists? Is it that they close ranks so as to present, perhaps unwittingly, a united front to an at times hostile higher education environment? Or are they simply nice people who will speak no ill of colleagues? Or do they not know their colleagues well enough to be specific? Whatever the reason, the faculty had little to say about one another, either positive or negative.

Holmes Group Membership

A second question that elicited little interest from interviewees was, "How does being/not being at a Holmes Group institution affect you?" With few exceptions, the question provoked a ho-hum response, whether the individuals were at Holmes Group-member institutions or not. Few reactions ranged beyond boredom with the question, mild petulance with the situation in which, as some stated it, a group of deans was telling others what to do, smug satisfaction with one's own institution and programs and a sense of déjà vu. Several individuals from non–Holmes Group institutions were totally indifferent to its existence. One male full professor said, "No, the Holmes Group doesn't excite me even though we went through the same thing 10 years ago." A female science educator at a state institution said, "Oh, I don't think I'd like to be at a Holmes Group institution. I like the freedom and the autonomy at a place like this."

The only person with much to say about the Holmes Group that was specific and detailed was a dean who had been very active in the process. He saw it as one means of promoting change. "I think the Holmes agenda culls ideas that have been around for a long, long time, puts them in a reformist mold, and says, 'let's get about the business of doing something.' It challenges everything from our relationship with the schools to the ranks for teachers." Yet the faculty whom I interviewed in that institution contended that the dean had already promoted most of the Holmes Group agenda some time before the formation of the group.

Several said it made no difference whether their institution belonged or not: "We're doing all that stuff anyway." "I don't think it's the Holmes Group membership. I think it was the agenda that the dean came here with. I think that what we were doing predated the Holmes Group." Some were irritated that a group of administrators were trying to tell all the teacher preparation faculty and institutions what to do. But in general, it clearly was not an issue that the individuals in this group wanted to spend much time or energy on.

It may be that reform agendas such as the Holmes Group initiative are rightly or wrongly perceived as administrator-led efforts not touching faculty on a day-to-day basis. In addition, older teacher-education faculty in the study have lived through several reform periods and seen little change. As one faculty member observed, "I've seen three reforms come and go in my time. Nothing changed much." Another commented, "It's what I do every day that matters, not what some national group tells me I should be doing." These faculty may perceive themselves as competent professionals not needing the goading from outsiders to perform. Certainly their remarks in their interviews suggest that they believe that they know what they are doing and that what they are doing is right.

The lack of interest in the Holmes Group work caused me to question some of my own exhortations to the profession that I had made in 1986 in an article entitled "The Professors and the Reports: A Time to Act." It did not appear that these faculty saw the Holmes activities as germane to their own work. Nor did they find the excitement that Zumwalt (1987) had forecast:

> The report holds the promise of sustained attention and resources devoted to teacher education in Holmes Group institutions. For teacher educators, long used to being considered second-class citizens by too many of their faculty colleagues, this indicates exciting times of collaborations in program development and research. (Ducharme, 1986b, p. 437)

In 1991 I wrote, "The Holmes Group briefly claimed public attention, but failed to speak out on some critical issues, to accomplish specific, discrete tasks, and to establish long-term, clearly identified goals" (p. 27). These interviewees perhaps sensed something early, namely, that the Holmes Group activities probably would not have much effect on their lives, that like many previous reform efforts it would wither away. The degree to which they were right remains to be seen. It is worth noting that they did not state their views of the Holmes Group and other reform efforts in a cynical way. It was not a case of, "Oh, I've seen this before, and I'm just going to wait it out." Rather, they simply believe in what they are doing, in the quality of the work at their institutions, and the ability of their students. And, as their remarks reveal, they do not see themselves as the second-class citizens that Zumwalt claims their faculty colleagues do.

Three Books

Finally, the question asking them what three books—from any categories they might choose—would they want their students to have read so as to "make them better teachers and better people" drew what were for me disappointing responses. As a person who has derived great meaning from imaginative works of literature, I am sure that I was hoping that there would be frequent citations of classic works of literature. Alas, such was not the case! Shakespeare's *Macbeth* received one nomination, and that was it for the Bard of Avon. Books receiving "votes" included *The Thread That Runs So True* (Stuart, 1949), *Up the Down Staircase* (Kaufman, 1965),

The Future of Man (Teilhard de Chardin, 1964), *The Saber-Tooth Curriculum* (Benjamin, 1939), *The Blackboard Jungle* (Hunter, 1954), *Sociology of Teaching* (Waller, 1932), *Will the Real Teacher Please Stand Up?* (Greer, 1972), *The Transformation of the School* (Cremin, 1961), *Horace's Compromise* (Sizer, 1984), *Future Shock* (Toffler, 1970), the Bible, and *Silent Spring* (Carson, 1962).

There were also several very vague answers containing references to an unnamed book; included in these answers were "something by Eric Erickson," "the Bloom book," "a fantastic history book," and the "handbook," which, upon questioning, turned out to be Wittrock's *Handbook of Research on Teaching*. Five interviewees, after thinking for several minutes and talking about the question, named no books or authors.

A typical initial response to the question was, "That's an interesting question," but some of the *answers* that followed were not very interesting: "I can't honestly think of anything." "I never thought about that before." "Come back in six months and ask me." "I read *about* books more than I read books." "I guess that I just can't answer that question." A female assistant professor noted, "Obviously, there are not a lot of books that I read that are ones where I'd say, 'Oh my God, this is the thing!' I would probably, oh, I would have them read a classic development book. I don't have specific one; there are two or three."

A male associate professor remarked on what they should read about rather than what they should read,

> If I could give students one thing, forget books, it would be this
> framework to problem solve. There is no book on this yet. Nobody
> is making the connections. Maybe I ought to do that. Maybe I
> would have them go into literature. Maybe any two pieces of litera-
> ture.

A male full professor at one point speculated, "Provincialism is probably the central problem in teacher education." Certainly the paucity of recommendations for texts might reinforce his observation. He then went on to comment about the *kind* of books he would want students to read, not the specific books.

> If I had to select a book, I'd select one that would challenge
> their paradigm. If whatever they're reading doesn't challenge
> their assumptions, it doesn't have much effect. I'd want them
> to read books that would help them appreciate the realms of
> meaning.

Clearly, these faculty do not generally carry in their heads the titles, authors, and contents of books that they would recommend to their colleagues and to their students. As I reflect on the responses to this question, I recognize that I was perhaps hoping that through the very general and open way in which I had asked it ("your own lifetime of reading of all kinds—personal, professional, or any other kind") would have prompted people to respond with books beyond the professional range. This was obviously a case of the researcher looking for what he wanted! As I was writing this chapter I recalled an essay "Liberal Arts in Teacher Education: The Perennial Challenge" (1980) in which I had argued that "Teacher educators without a liberal education are boring" (p. 10). I also commented on the personal value of reading broadly.

> My education had prepared me well for broadening my definition of what it is to be human. For example, when I read *A Portrait of the Artist as a Young Man*, I experienced growth in awareness of what it is to be human. I had little sense of an Irish tradition in America or Ireland; I had never been educated by Jesuits, never walked the streets of Dublin nor argued the merits of the rebel Parnell. (Before I read this book, the only Parnell I knew was Mel Parnell, a Red Sox pitcher.) To read the book was to experience yearnings I had never felt, to imagine a familial pattern I had never experienced, to feel politics as a matter of everyday life, a phenomenon foreign to my youth. At the same time, the book made me conscious of another who had shared my own desires for identity, uniqueness, rebellion, heroism, and love. This book and hundreds of others immeasurably broadened my understanding of the great world outside me and vastly enhanced my smaller inside world. (p. 7)

I may have been unconsciously looking for responses related to the sentiment of the above remarks. I believe so strongly in the power of imaginative literature to enliven the imagination and broaden the vision of readers that I was wanting to impute to others my own views. Yet in fairness to the interviewees, their remarks throughout often evidenced an awareness of the need to feed the soul, albeit generally absent a particular reference by which to do so. The question, however, provoked a long-term response in at least one individual who recently communicated to me that "It still bothers me that I couldn't come up with three books."

A current theme about researchers and their work is that they often seek information and data that pertain greatly to their own lives and interests. As I review the interview protocol I developed and used, I think the theme applies well to my study, particularly so to the "three books" question.

REFLECTIVE CONCLUSIONS

Faculty Integrity

The faculty in this study are individuals of great integrity. Their comments repeatedly stressed their commitment to the work that they do, respect for their colleagues and the students, a concern for quality, and a belief in young people. Speaking of his obligations to his profession, a mature full professor noted, "We owe something to this state; we have to give something back."

While I earlier expressed mild befuddlement over the faculty reluctance to comment in any detail on their colleagues, the unwillingness also bespeaks of personal integrity. In a contentious age, the presence of people of civility among prospective teachers cannot be a bad thing.

Integrity cuts across the ages of the faculty. For some of the older faculty integrity found expression in institutional loyalty, commitment to the field, and to professionalism. The younger faculty generally share some of these views, and in part because of their different doctoral preparation, are also more committed to the development of knowledge through personal research and scholarship.

Belief in Their Work and a Sense of Responsibility

The faculty speak much of the importance and value of what they do. They talk about the conditions in the schools today and how prospective teachers must be prepared to cope and thrive in changing environments. "I worry that I haven't prepared them well enough." Although they see certain things as constants in schools—the needs for competency, solid educational background, care for young people—they also recognize that the schools are changing, that society is changing. And they believe very strongly that they must play a part in this important process. "We must prepare the best teachers that we can." These individuals take their responsibilities very seriously.

They not only believe in their work, they also believe in themselves. While not hubris driven, the faculty in this study generally spoke with a quiet confidence about what they do, about a sense of their own importance. Some of the older faculty had been through several periods of growth and decline, through times of intense criticism, through others questioning their work. But their words and the tones with which they spoke rarely displayed feelings of inadequacy or lack of acceptance. The younger faculty were eager to contribute to their profession, pleased to be working in significant efforts. None of them resembled the faculty whom

I had described a number of years ago as not welcome in higher education (1986a). As the faculty member quoted in Chapter 6 noted, "Deep down I feel very positive." It was pleasant to be proven wrong in at least the instances of the faculty in this study.

I suspect there are several reasons for the level of comfort that they expressed. First, they responded in a time of stability in their lives and in their institutions; nearly all, save one or two recently appointed faculty, felt secure in their positions, and the fiscal crises of the 1990s had not yet hit. Second, they like their students and respect their unit administration. "We have great students here." "The dean is rigorous but fair." Third, I asked questions that often led to positive recollections. The only query that invited negative speculation was that about the frustration in their work. However, whatever the reasons, these 34 individuals were extraordinarily positive.

Research in the Schools

Some of the faculty are directly connected with the lower schools through the work they do in them, often in cooperation with teachers. The work underway by interviewees includes studying the learning of the handicapped, attempts to improve the teaching of science and mathematics, ethnographic studies of classrooms, development of curricula in content areas such as English and language arts, studies of the work of beginning teachers, and work with teacher groups. It is ironic that while the group as a whole showed little interest in the Holmes Group and its work, many of them are doing things that are part of the Holmes Group agenda, such as conducting research in schools with teachers. This work and related activities argue that the faculty are knowledgeable about conditions in the schools, a necessary attribute for professional educators attempting to prepare young people to teach.

Broad Range of Responsibility

The growing number of activities of these individuals, including the conducting of research in schools, appears to be resulting in what may become an unmanageable range of responsibilities; they may be overcommitting themselves. These faculty, like so many in SCDEs, stand poised between academe and the lower schools. Many do not only the work of higher education, including committee membership, curriculum development, research and scholarship, and service, but also relate to the schools through inservice work, intern supervision, and continuing education courses. Their calendars are nearly always full. They are extraordinarily busy and responsible. Their consciences and their competencies may be forcing them into what could become intolerable expectations.

At Home in Higher Education

These faculty appear to be content with their places of employment; they like many things about higher education. As I indicated in Chapter 3, they find most aspects of their work to be both challenging and rewarding. Although one cannot generalize from this study about the whole teacher education population, these faculty are generally actively involved in the life of higher education. Several sit in key governance roles, a condition that augurs well for the life of their academic units in the broader institution. I find this to be refreshingly in contrast with what Agne and I (Ducharme & Agne, 1982, 1989) and Lanier and Little (1986) concluded about teacher education faculty, namely, that they were not very active in the governance of their institutions. Faculty in other units may continue to think ill of them, as Clark (1987), Zumwalt (1987), and others suggest, but if such is the case, it appears to upset very few.

Need for Self-Scrutiny

As I indicated in Chapter 6, significant discrepancies appear to exist between males and females with respect to roles, duties, degree of field supervision, salary, rank and tenure, and feelings of respect. It is not insignificant that, with two exceptions, only females discussed these matters. The professoriate must engage in significant self-scrutiny and determine the degree to which these conditions prevail, and if they do, act. I commented on the civility of these faculty members, a civility that leads to smooth relationships and what is perceived to be a harmonious group. Perhaps these conditions suggest a need to move beyond civility.

One need not be a militant to note that there is a contradiction between a commitment to prepare a professional cadre of students, a majority of whom are female, to become powerful teachers and effective advocates for youth, and a condition in which the female faculty are in roles and positions implying an inequity between the genders. As Kluender and I (1990) observed, "Women may publish less because they are often asked to assume supervisory responsibilities at a disproportionate level, and they teach more" (p. 47). The students themselves will subsequently teach in schools that will be largely headed by male principals. As conditions stand, they may have had few role models of their own gender leading them to question and challenge the system.

FURTHER WORK

Nearly all studies in education never end. The very inquiry itself leads to more unanswered questions. This study is no exception. As I was completing my round of interviews and in the intervening months as I typed the transcripts and studied them, I often thought of matters needing further examination or ways in which the study itself might be changed somewhat to study different but related issues. The following are a few of the matters that still seem relevant to me.

• *A Sharper, More Focused Inquiry.* It would be interesting and worthwhile to focus on a singular aspect of the teacher-education professorial life, for example, the work of university-based teacher educators when they are in the lower schools supervising interns or performing service activities. The RATE studies provide excellent data on the amount of time and percentage of load that faculty give to field supervision, but there is little extant material on precisely what it is they do when they are there, what use they make of what they do, the reactions of those with whom they work, and so forth. A close, detailed study of several faculty as they visit and work in lower-school settings, noting carefully their activities, interviewing them, and studying those with whom they are working would be of immense importance.

• *Specific Types of Institutions.* In this study I sought a range of institutions, from a rural four-year private college to a large state flagship university. It would be of value to conduct a study at an essentially urban, nonresidential university or a historically black institution, or a private college and focus on the lives of teacher education within very carefully limited environments Perhaps one would find that the professional life differs in these very focused institutions. As the reader notes, I did not find many differences between the smallest of the institutions and the largest.

• *Broader Definition of Teacher Educator.* I indicated that I had limited my study to full-time university-based teacher educators. I believe this to be a necessary boundary on the population of teacher educators for this study. Yet we know that others in the lower schools, in state departments of education, in private consulting, in federal programs, and elsewhere all do teacher education. Again, a study of these individuals would further illuminate the matter of who teaches teachers, what are they like, and what they do. Finally, it would enable one to define more clearly how the roles may differ, given their sites.

• *Shadow Studies.* With any of the above and with other possibilities for subjects, one could conduct shadow studies of those in the role and describe fully the total days of the individuals. Such studies would provide more in the way of what individual teacher education faculty do. Gideonse (1989) did something of this nature when he asked faculty through their use of journals to record their daily activities. It is an important contribution, but remains self-reporting. A shadow study would provide fuller data.

A LAST WORD

"My days are so exciting." This sentiment is one all faculty might wish to be able to say as the various stages of their careers unfold. As I look back over the interviews, the faculty with whom I spoke, my ruminations over their words in the following months, and all that occurred in-between, I remain struck with the decency, integrity, and the value of these faculty. Oh, they might have disappointed me in their "failure" to fulfill my hopes for a rich collection of titles of imaginative literature that future teachers should read. But their interest in their work, their concern for quality, their high hopes for their students, their thoughtfulness, and their zest for life more than fulfill hopes one might have for standards about those who work with the young to help them prepare to be teachers.

In much of my previous writing about the professoriate, I and my frequent co-authors often wrote about the problems and weaknesses in the lives and careers of teacher education faculty and education faculty in general. We wrote of the relatively low socioeconomic backgrounds, their occasionally questionable academic credentials, and their frequently low reputation with faculty in other disciplines. It was refreshing to listen to and analyze the remarks of these teacher educators who, for whatever reasons, do not fit those molds or, if they do, live and talk in such manner as to surmount the effects of their pasts and others' opinions of them. It is always good when the future shows positive changes from the past; clearly, these people's lives do so. Contentment reigns for some: "I think the professorial life is great. It's a great life. I don't work. My father *worked*. It's a good life; the life in professional life is very good."

The future for the teacher education faculty is bright. There are, first of all, the numbers of people in the profession who fit the profiles of those in this study. There are also those who are preparing for the roles in doctoral programs. The likelihood is that they will continue to raise the level of talent and performance of the teacher education professoriate. They will maintain and perhaps enhance the place of teacher education faculty in the "academic firmament" to which Wisniewski and I (1989a, p. 147) referred.

References

Aisenberg, N., & Harrington, M. (1988). *Women of academe: Outsiders in the sacred grove*. Amherst: University of Massachusetts Press.

Allison, C. (1989). Early professors of education: Three case studies. In R. Wisniewski & E. Ducharme (Eds.), *The professors of teaching: An inquiry* (pp. 29–51). Albany: State University of New York Press.

Bagley, A. (Ed.). (1975). *The professors of education: An assessment of conditions*. Minneapolis: Society of Professors of Education, College of Education, University of Minnesota.

Benjamin, H. (1939). *Saber-tooth curriculum, including other lectures in the history of paleolithic education*. New York: McGraw-Hill.

Borrowman, M. (1956). *Teacher education in America: A documentary history*. New York, Teachers College Bureau of Publications.

Brittingham, B. (1986). Faculty development in teacher education. *Journal of Teacher Education, 37*(3), 2–5.

Broudy, H. (1972). *The real world of the public schools*. New York: Harcourt Brace Jovanovich.

Carnegie Forum on Education and the Economy. (1986). *A nation prepared: Teachers for the 21st century*. New York: Carnegie Forum.

Carson, R. (1962). *Silent spring*. Boston: Houghton Mifflin.

Carter, H. (1984). Teachers of teachers. In L. Katz & J. Raths (Eds.), *Advances in teacher education* (Vol. 1, pp. 125–143). Norwood, NJ: Ablex.

Clark, B. (1987). *The academic life: Small worlds, different world*. Princeton, NJ: The Carnegie Foundation for the Advancement of Teaching.

Clark, D. (1978). *Research and development productivity in educational organizations* (Occasional Paper No. 41). Columbus: National Center for Research in Vocational Education, Ohio State University.

Clifford, G., & Guthrie, G. (1988). *Ed school*. Chicago: University of Chicago Press.

Cohen, R. K. (1991). *A lifetime of teaching: Portraits of five veteran high school teachers*. New York: Teachers College Press.

Cremin, L. (1961). *The transformation of the school: Progressivism in American education*. New York: Knopf.

Davies, R. (1983). *The Deptford trilogy*. New York: Penguin.

Davies, R. (1986). *The Salterton trilogy.* New York: Penguin.

Doyle, W. (1986). Classroom organization and management. In M. Wittrock (Ed.), *Handbook of research on teaching* (3rd ed., pp. 392–431). New York: Macmillan.

Ducharme, E. (1980). Liberal arts in teacher education: The perennial challenge, *Journal of Teacher Education, 31*(3), 7–12.

Ducharme, E. (1986a). Teacher educators: Description and analysis. In J. Raths & L. Katz (Eds.), *Advances in teacher education* (Vol. 2, pp. 39–60). Norwood, NJ: Ablex.

Ducharme, E. (1986b). The professors and the reports: A time to act. *Journal of Teacher Education, 37*(3), 51–56.

Ducharme, E. (1986c). *Teacher educators: What do we know?* Washington, DC: ERIC Clearinghouse on Teacher Education, American Association of Colleges for Teacher Education.

Ducharme, E. (1987). Developing existing education faculty. In C. Magrath & R. Egbert (Eds.), *Strengthening teacher education* (pp. 71–86). San Francisco: Jossey-Bass.

Ducharme, E. (1991). The Holmes Group watch: Is it over? *Impact on Instructional Improvement, 23*(3), 26–29.

Ducharme, E., & Agne, R. (1982). The education professoriate: A research-based perspective. *Journal of Teacher Education, 33*(6), 30–36.

Ducharme, E., & Agne, R. (1986). Professors of education: Beasts of burden, facilitators, or academicians. *Journal of Human Behavior and Analysis, 4*(2), 1–9.

Ducharme, E., & Agne, R. (1989). Professors of education: Uneasy residents of academe. In R. Wisniewski & E. Ducharme (Eds.), *The professors of teaching: An inquiry* (pp. 67–86). Albany: State University of New York Press.

Ducharme, E., & Kluender, M. (1990). The RATE study: The faculty. *Journal of Teacher Education, 44*(4), 45–49.

Fuller, F., & Bown, O. (1975). Becoming a teacher. In K. Ryan (Ed.), *Teacher education* (74th yearbook of the National Society for the Study of Education, Pt. 2, pp. 25–52). Chicago: University of Chicago Press.

Gideonse, H. (1989). The uses of time: Evocation of an ethos. In R. Wisniewski & E. Ducharme (Eds.), *The professors of teaching: An inquiry* (pp. 119–133). Albany: State University of New York Press.

Glesne, G., & Peshkin, A. (1992). *Becoming qualitative researchers: An introduction.* White Plains, NY: Longman.

Goodlad, J. (1990). *Teachers for our nation's schools.* San Francisco: Jossey-Bass.

Goodlad, J., Soder, R., & Sirotnik, K. (1990a). (Eds.). *Places where teachers are taught.* San Francisco: Jossey-Bass.

Goodlad, J., Soder, R., & Sirotnik, K. (1990b). (Eds.). *The moral dimensions of teaching.* San Francisco: Jossey-Bass.

Greer, M. C. (1972). *Will the real teacher please stand up? A primer in humanistic education.* New York: Goodyear.

Hazlett, J. (1989). Education professors: The centennial of an identity crisis. In R. Wisniewski & E. Ducharme (Eds.), *The professors of teaching: An inquiry* (pp. 110–128). Albany: State University of New York Press.

Holmes Group. (1986). *Tomorrow's teachers: A report of the Holmes Group*. East Lansing, MI: The Holmes Group.

Howey, K. (1982). Teacher education in the United States: Trends and issues. *The Teacher Educator, 27*(4), 3–11.

Howey, K., Yarger, S., & Joyce, B. (1978). *Improving teacher education*. Washington, DC: Association of Teacher Educators.

Howey, K., & Zimpher, N. (1989). *Profiles of preservice education: Inquiries into the nature of programs*. Albany: State University of New York Press.

Howey, K., & Zimpher, N. (1990). Professors and deans of education. In W. R. Houston (Ed.), *Handbook of research on teacher education* (pp. 349–370). New York: Macmillan.

Hunter, E. (1954). *The blackboard jungle*. New York: Dell.

Jeruchim, J., & Shapior, P. (1992). *Women, mentoring, and success*. New York: Fawcett Columbine.

Judge, H. (1982). *American graduate schools of education: A view from abroad*. New York: Ford Foundation.

Kaufman, B. (1965). *Up the down staircase*. Englewood Cliffs, NJ: Prentice-Hall.

Koerner, J. (1963). *The miseducation of American teachers*. Boston: Houghton Mifflin.

Ladd, E. C., Jr., & Lipset, S. (1975). *The divided academy: Professors and politics*. New York: McGraw-Hill.

Lanier, J., & Little, J. (1986). Research in teacher education. In M. Wittrock (Ed.), *Handbook of research on teaching* (3rd ed., pp. 527–569). New York: Macmillan.

Lasley, T. (1986). Editorial. *Journal of Teacher Education, 37*(3), inside cover.

Lawson, H. (1990). Constraints on the professional service of education faculty. *Journal of Teacher Education, 44*(4), 45–49.

Lortie, D. C. (1975). *Schoolteacher: A sociological study*. Chicago: University of Chicago Press.

Murray, F., & Fallon, D. (1990). *The reform of teacher education for the 21st century: Project 30 year one report*. Newark: University of Delaware, Project 30.

National Commission on Excellence in Education. (1983). *A nation at risk: The imperative for educational reform*. Washington, DC: U.S. Department of Education.

Palmer, J. (1985). Teacher education: A perspective from a major public university. In C. Case & W. Matthes (Eds.), *Colleges of education: Perspectives on their future* (pp. 51–70). Berkeley, CA: McCutchan.

Popkewitz, T. (Ed.). (1987). *Critical studies in teacher education: Its folklore, theory and practice*. New York: Falmer Press.

RATE I. Teaching teachers: Facts and figures. (1987). Washington, DC: American Association of Colleges for Teacher Education.

RATE II. Teaching teachers: Facts and figures. (1988). Washington, DC: American Association of Colleges for Teacher Education.

RATE III. Teaching teachers: Facts and figures. (1989). Washington, DC: American Association of Colleges for Teacher Education.

RATE IV. Teaching teachers: Facts and figures. (1990). Washington, DC: American Association of Colleges for Teacher Education.

RATE V. Teaching teachers: Facts and figures. (1991). Washington, DC: American Association of Colleges for Teacher Education.

Rudolph, F. (1962). *The American college and university.* New York: Knopf.

Russell, S., Cox, R., Williamson, C., Boismier, J., Javitz, H., Fairweather, J., & Zimbler, L. (1990). *Faculty in higher education institutions, 1988.* Washington, DC: U.S. Department of Education.

Sarton, May. (1961). *The small room.* New York: W. W. Norton.

Schneider, B. (1987). Tracing the provenance of teacher educators. In T. Popkewitz (Ed.), *Critical studies in teacher education: Its folklore, theory and practice* (pp. 211–241). New York: Falmer Press.

Schwebel, M. (1989). The new priorities and the education faculty. In R. Wisniewski & E. Ducharme (Eds.), *The professors of teaching: An inquiry* (pp. 52–66). Albany: State University of New York Press.

Sikes, P., Measor, L., & Woods, P. (1985). *Teacher careers: Crises and continuities.* London: Falmer Press.

Simeone, A. (1987). *Academic women: Working towards equality.* South Hadley, MA: Begin & Garvey Publishers, Inc.

Sizer, T. (1984). *Horace's compromise.* Boston: Houghton-Mifflin.

Soder, R. (1990). How faculty members feel when the reward structure changes. *Phi Delta Kappan, 71*(9), 702–709.

Spencer, D. A. (1986). *Contemporary women teachers: Balancing school and home.* New York: Longman.

Stuart, J. (1949). *The thread that runs so true.* New York: Charles Scribner's Sons.

Teilhard de Chardin, P. (1964). *The future of man.* New York: Harper and Row.

Terkel, S. (1970). *Hard times: An oral history of the great depression.* New York: Pantheon.

Terkel, S. (1974). *Working: People talk about what they do all day and how they feel about what they do.* New York: Pantheon.

Toffler, A. (1970). *Future shock.* New York: Random House.

Troyer, M. (1986). *Journal of Teacher Education, 37*(3), 6–11.

Waller, W. (1932). *The sociology of teaching.* New York: Russell and Co.

Warren, D. (Ed.). (1989). *American teachers: Histories of a profession at work.* New York: Macmillan.

Wilson, L. (1979). *American academics: Then and now.* New York: Oxford University Press.

Wisniewski, R. (1989). The ideal professor of education. In R. Wisniewski & E. Ducharme (Eds.), *The professors of teaching: An inquiry* (pp. 134–146). Albany: State University of New York Press.

Wisniewski, R., & Ducharme, E. (1989a). Where we stand. In R. Wisniewski & E. Ducharme (Eds.), *The professors of teaching: An inquiry* (pp. 147–162). Albany: State University of New York Press.

Wisniewski, R., & Ducharme, E. (Eds.). (1989b). *The professors of teaching: An inquiry.* Albany: State University of New York Press.

Zeichner, K. (1986). Individual and institutional influences on the development of teacher perspectives. In J. Raths & L. Katz (Eds.), *Advances in teacher education* (Vol. 2, pp. 135–157). Norwood, NJ: Ablex.

Zumwalt, K. (1987). *Tomorrow's teachers:* Tomorrow's work. *Teachers College Record, 88*(3), 436–441.

Index

About the Author

Edward Ducharme is Ellis Levitt Distinguished Professor of Education at Drake University, Des Moines, Iowa, where he has taught since 1991. He currently co-chairs the Department of Teacher Education and Curriculum Studies. He holds degrees from Colby College, Harvard University, and Teachers College, Columbia University, where he received his doctorate in 1968. He taught high school English for seven years before teaching at Trinity College, Washington, DC, and the University of Vermont, where he taught for eighteen years and chaired academic departments.

He has published widely on teacher education, higher education, faculty development, and public education. In addition to over forty articles, he has authored or co-authored five chapters in professional books and co-edited several collections of writings, including *The Professors of Teaching*. He currently serves as co-editor of the *Journal of Teacher Education*.